THIS BOOK IS FOR YO

- you want to use the ideas to think for yourself and renew your whole attitude to work

- you want not just to learn, but to learn how to learn, life long

The social reality around us is a pattern we ourselves have constructed. It is less fact and solid foundation than conjecture. Capitalism especially is what different cultures conceive it to mean. It is not "freedom" assured by some divine, global mechanism but a set of suppositions and rules we have constructed for better or for worse which should enter into dialogue with one another to find better solutions. A current crisis in this capitalism, similar to Brexit, gives us a chance to reconceive. We need to ask what an economy is for, and this means being "radical", less in the sense of socialism, than in going to the roots (radix) of what it means to create wealth. We need a moral science of economic development around which whole nations and regions can cohere.

This book tunnels down to our deepest and most basic assumptions and asks if these are not overdue for revision. Could thinking in a different way make work a form of self-fulfilment? To innovate is among the purest pleasures known to man. Can an entire culture find purpose and direction in what it supplies and consumes? One of the surprises in this book is just how many corporations and new movements have found that higher goals of human betterment are not only possible but morale-boosting and profitable to pursue. Profit is a needed fuel, not a destination, a means of expanding what you do, not an aim in itself. Economists may be right, money is at any one moment of time, scarce. But over periods of time, ideas are NOT scarce and the more of these you, have the more you can generate. And these turn from insubstantial mental constructs into valuable and substantial products and services. This book is dedicated to multiple ideas and harvesting these in lives lived to the hilt.

WHAT PEOPLE ARE SAYING ABOUT THE WORK OF THESE AUTHORS

TOM PETERS

"This is a masterpiece...." (comment on Riding the Waves of Culture)

WILL HUTTON

"An invaluable and path-breaking overview of capitalism's many hues." The Guardian (review of The Seven Cultures of Capitalism).

VINCE CABLE

"This is a major piece of work and is strongly recommended to anyone trying to understand contemporary business..." (comment on The Seven Cultures...)

CHARLES HANDY

"Authoritative, insightful and stimulating..." (comment on The Seven Cultures)

WARREN BENNIS

"Illuminates the darkness around the elusive concept of "culture" with a rich theoretical texture, and with powerful illustrations." (comment on Building Cross Cultural Competence)

PETER SENGE

"Profound, engaging, important, a wealth of illustration. A memorable contribution to systems dynamics." (comment on Corporate Culture: Vicious and Virtuous Circles)

MARSHALL GOLDSMITH

"Fons Trompenaars is a world authority on cross-cultural innovation..." (comment on Riding the Whirlwind)

MIHALY CSIKSZENTMIHALYI

"...A brilliant study that could benefit anyone responsible for the management of international high tech teams and those interested in group creativity." (Comment on The Titans of Saturn)

JOHN NAISBITT

"An important and brilliant book. With deep insights into China." (comment on Nine cultures of Capitalism)

R EDWARD FREEMAN

"It is a pleasure to read a book by two thinkers who actually understand how business works." (comment on Nine Cultures of Capitalism)

DOUG RAUCH

"the chapter on Conscious Capitalism is worth the price of the book alone." (comment on Nine Cultures...)

EDWARD DE BONO

"An intriguing book which explores the habits and methods of thinking across a wide range of cultures. It emphasises once again that traditional Western thinking is only one set of habits." (comment on Mastering the Infinite Game)

SIR PETER PARKER

"A necessary revelation….a fine piece of radicalism, beyond left and right, reconciling heaven and hell. In fact I keep thinking of William Blake's line "Opposition is true friendship." (Comment on Mastering the Infinite Game)

ROBERT F BALES

"An eye-opener for me …this book is so circumstantial, so concrete, co comprehensive, so well-presented ….that I felt I had known almost nothing about this subject before."   (comment on Mastering the Infinite Game)

GREGORY BATESON

"Much of it is very good….and some of it is brilliant." (comment on Sane Asylum: Inside the Delancey Street Foundation)

ABRAHAM MASLOW

"This is a brilliant and creative man. I was very much impressed." (comment on Radical Man: the process of psycho-social development)

SILVAN S TOMKINS

"A fine and passionate work…"   (comment on Radical Man)

MILTON KOTLER

"For the first time we have a brilliant psychological theory in support of self-determined community institutions." (Comment on From Poverty to Dignity)

About the Authors

Professor Charles Hampden-Turner has a doctorate from the Harvard Business School and graduated from Trinity College, Cambridge and worked in the USA for 21 years. He was Senior Research Associate at the Judge Business School at Cambridge University for eighteen years. He is author of Maps of the Mind New York: Macmillan, a Book of the Month Club selection. He was Goh Tjoe Kok Distinguished Visiting Professor to Nanyang Technological University in Singapore 2002-2003 and Hutchinson Visiting Scholar to China in 2004. He is a past winner of the Douglas McGregor Memorial Award and was the Royal Dutch Shell Senior Research Fellow at the London Business School. In 1984 he co-founded Trompenaars Hampden-Turner, the cross-cultural consulting company with his partner Fons. He is the author of twenty-two books, eight with Fons. Their books have been translated into twenty languages. Charles has won Guggenheim and Rockefeller Fellowships.

Professor Fons Trompenaars is an organizational theorist, management consultant and best-selling author, well-known for his seven-dimensional model of national business cultures. Riding the Waves of Culture (written with Hampden-Turner) has sold one third of a million copies. He was awarded the International Professional Practice Area Research Award by the American Society for Training and Development. In 2011 HR Magazine voted him among the world's 20 top international thinkers. He has been elected to the Thinkers50 Hall of Fame for management scholars. He is a professor at the Free University of Amsterdam and where he heads a course on Servant Leadership. He was until recently a partner at KPMG in Amstelveen. His latest book is 100+ Management Models which has won a prize in Malaysia. Until recently he had a column in the Dutch language edition of the Financial Times which described him as "a new star in of the world's management seminar circuit."

Professor Linda O'Riordan is a reflective practitioner with a doctorate from the University of Bradford in the UK. Her research interest lies in stakeholder management and responsible entrepreneurship focusing on sustainable approaches for business in society. Her academic activities include lecturing on Business Studies and International Management at leading Universities, and she is the Director of a Research Competence Centre for Corporate Social Responsibility at the FOM University of Applied Sciences in Germany. Her work has appeared in internationally renowned research publications and she is the author, editor, and reviewer of various academic books and peer-reviewed journals. Her latest highly acclaimed book is Managing Sustainable Stakeholder Relationships: Corporate Approaches to Responsible Management. Before becoming an academic, she gained business and consultancy experience from working in industry. Some of her former employers include Accenture, UCB-Schwarz Pharma, and the Government of Ireland (Irish Food Board/Bord Bia).

ACKNOWLEDGEMENTS

Acknowledgements always make us feel humble and wonder whether it would not be fairer to attribute "our" work to whole networks of people. It reminds us that independence is often an illusion. We are interdependent and have just one end of scores of relationships, through which knowledge flows. The first-named author owes most to his partner Fons Trompenaars, who has run our consultancy since 1984 and paid him from its proceeds. CMH-T cannot organize a proverbial paper bag. We are also grateful to Phyllis Stewart, the one person who knows on what plane Trompenaars, is currently flying and how and when to locate him. She is our sheet-anchor. Barbara Blokpoel collected, organized, edited, filed and commissioned many of the pictures in this book. Whenever CMH-T got lost in the Netherlands, she would magically appear amidst dense crowds to rescue him.

Talking of pictures, we owe much to the genius of David Lewis. We hope this book brings him the fame he so much deserves. While we think up the pictures and their messages, his wicked sense of humour saves us from solemnity and we often reflect that the joke may be partly on us. He spent hours drawing at the Royal Society for the Arts and his artwork drew interested spectators. CMH-T owes to Robert Eddison, his room-mate at Trinity College at Cambridge, an introduction to Chris Day, the Managing Director of Filament Publishing, who instantly saw what was intended in this book. We are flattered by his personal intervention as to how it should be presented and to his optimism about its prospects. We also owe much to the forbearance and patience of Olivia Eisinger, our editor. We are not masters of detail and we change our minds too often. If this book approaches coherence, thank her.

The kind words of trusted friends and fellow authors mean much to us. Among these are Charles Handy, Henry Mintzberg, Nancy Adler, Alan Barrel, Edward R Freeman, Clayton Christensen, Mimi Silbert, Peter Hiscocks, Ed Schein, Napier Collyns, John Cleese, Milton Bennett, Ida Castiglioni,

John Naisbitt, Vincent Cable, Tom Cummings, Hermann Simon, Raymond Madden, Tom Peters, Arie de Geus, Martin Gillo, David K Hurst, Ray Abelin, Peter Woolliams, Jay Ogilvy, Wendy Smith, Linda Putman, Edward de Bono, Marianne Lewis, Sylvia van de Bunt, Pi-Shen Seet, Cheenu Srinivasan and Raymond Madden. Many of those who influenced us most are now dead and we have tried to bring them briefly to life again in what we write, so their influence survives. These include, in the order of their influence, Gregory Bateson, Abraham Maslow, Rollo May, James McGregor Burns, Douglas McGregor, Chris Argyris, Donald Schon, Warren Bennis, Nevitt Sanford, Fritz Roethlisberger, Elliott Jacques, Carl Rogers, Adam Curle, John S Seeley, Richard Farson, John Maher, Silvan Tompkins, Sir Peter Parker, James Mitchell, Robert F Bales, George C Lodge, John Stopford and Tan Teng-Kee.

We owe much to three institutions, The Big Innovation Centre whose ideas we originally researched for this book and the Institute for Leadership and Management which has supported our work. Prof. Birgitte Andersen, Head of BIC, shared her ideas with us and enthused over our work in general, as did Niki Iliadis, Innovative Policy and Foresight manager. If female empowerment is to be like this, we look forward to it. Some of the better ideas in this book could be triggered by the BIC but the authors are entirely to blame for the remainder. The Institute for Leadership and Management has supported a much more comprehensive encyclopaedia of leadership published later this year, from which this book draws. We are indebted to Kate Cooper, Phil James, John Galvin and Beverly Hogg among others for their support and we hope these books will help them. The Institute for Manufacturing at Cambridge University and its annexe for pensioners has allowed CMH-T to stay in touch with contemporary scholarship and he is especially indebted to Yongjiang Shi, Chander Velu and Tim Minshall.

Finally we give thanks to our families, to Shelley Hampden-Turner and our sons Michael and Hanbury, to Penelope, our grand-daughter, who sketched the picture of the Unicorn company and Charlie. Let them all last longer than this book!

The senior author would like to give thanks to his family who put up with his preoccupation.

Join in the conversation!

Our mentor, Gregory Bateson, used to say that there was no form of communication superior to a conversation, preferably face to face, but otherwise by Skype or on-line. In conversations you can tell the other that the very question is mistaken, that the premise is wrong. You can re-define the whole topic. In inquiries claiming to be scientific, like questionnaires, you are often trapped in the mistaken alternatives of the Other and cannot escape. So how can you join us in conversations about the ideas in this book? If sales are modest you have the e-mails of the current authors, but if sales are better than this, then it may not be possible for us to answer you without ceasing to be able to work or to write! In such a case the answer is to join the network of those who appreciate this book and allow your messages to be passed on to the various authors according to the priority in each case.

Clearly it is high priority to take initiatives suggested in this book, especially in the UK, the Netherlands and in Germany where its three authors reside and we would love to help you make these succeed. We stand ready to do so. It is also important to explain in more detail what we propose and opportunities to speak, preferably paid, are welcome as are invitations to participate in what you plan to do. It is clearly lower priority to help you get published your dissertation on Criteria for Promotion in the Mexican Navy , or respond to suggestions of where we should shove our ideas. Were you to approach us via the networks to which we are connected, such messages might be given their requisite priority before being passed on to us. You can approach us via our publisher, Filament which is in Croydon, via the Big Innovation Centre, close to Westminster in London, or via The Institute for Leadership and Management in Tamworth, UK. Or via our consulting arm Trompenaars Hampden-Turner. You might in this way succeed in enlisting the support of persons at that address as well as ours and informing them of opportunities . The two co-authors are in FOM in Essen, Germany and in Amsterdam in the Netherlands and it might be better to contact them, depending on what you want done, where.

We are connected to a Blog, which for a limited period of time will be active. Were this to get too abusive we would cease however and in such circumstances you will have to approach us by indirection via the addresses below.

For Charles Hampden-Turner   chuckht@aol.com   He lives in Cambridge, UK
                              charleshampdenturnersenior@gmail.com
For Fons Trompenaars   fons@thtconsulting.com He lives in Amsterdam
For Linda O'Riordan   linda.oriordan@t-online.de She lives in Essen, Germany

APPROACH THE NETWORKS

Filament Publishing   www.FilamentPublishing.com   16 Croydon Rd, Waddon, Croydon, Surrey CR0 4PA Tel. 44(0) 20 8688 2598

Big Innovation Centre   www.biginnovationcentre.com   20 Victoria Street, London SW1H 0NF Tel. 44(0) 20 3713 4036

The Institute for Leadership and Management www.InstituteLM.com   Pacific House, Relay Point, Tamworth B 77 5 PA Tel. 44 (0) 1543 266 866

Trompenaars Hampden-Turner Culture for Business www.thtconsulting.com Achillesstraat 89 1076 PX Amsterdam, the Netherlands Tel. 31 (0) 20301 6666

Linda O'Riordan   linda.oriordan@t-online.de FOM University of Applied Science Leimkugelstrasse 6 45141 ESSEN   Tel. 49 (0)201 81004-0

DEDICATIONS FROM THE AUTHORS

CHARLES HAMPDEN-TURNER

Charles would like to dedicate this book to the Delancey Street Foundation in San Francisco and its two founders Mimi Silbert and John Maher – the latter sadly died while still young but the former has persevered and is my heroine. It taught me about the amazing unity that can grow out of diversity. What was I doing, thousands of miles from home, a graduate of Cambridge with a doctorate in business from Harvard, in a half-way house for ex-convicts and drug addicts? Yet those two years changed my life. I was exposed to people whose lives were sheer wretchedness, yet emerged with enough hope to last a life-time. If these people could turn their lives around, there was surely hope for us all. I had always been on the side of the under-dog but that particular kennel had begun to stink, the War on Poverty had atrophied and I was fighting despair. But when I fully engaged the members I realized that I could not have withstood the ordeals they had suffered and my admiration grew.

Quite suddenly ideas that I had been taught were poles apart, public and private, poor and rich, intellect and emotion, business and social relationships, Harvard and St Quentin, the culture of criminality and how to transform it, money and caring, critical detachment and passionate engagement, all came together in a new integrity that has sustained me ever since. There was one session of marathon group therapy that lasted three days and two sleepless nights. It began in sheer hilarity at the stupidity of life-styles, the thief crawling through the window who fell into the bath-water and was menaced by a bath-brush until the police arrived. It ended in tragedy for those who did not laugh at themselves in time. It culminated in a story of the death of a baby born to an addicted mother, after hours of agony. My two sons were born in the months before and the months after this narrative.

Never in my life had I realized just how lucky I was. It is not until you have descended into hell that you understand what heaven is. For value lies in the strongest contrasts as this book will show. It was Martin Luther King who said that until you discover something for which you would be prepared to die, you have not truly lived. His speech was played in the last minutes of the group therapy. We too, had a dream and it was coming true as we awoke.

Linda O'Riordan

I dedicate this book to my Grandfather, Thomas Heaps, who understood that the greatest wisdom of all is first to love. In the hope that I can pass this spirit on to my son, Liam

Fons Trompenaars

For my wife, Cens

CAPITALISM IN CRISIS
WHAT'S GONE WRONG
AND HOW CAN WE FIX IT?

HOW TO MOVE TOWARDS A CIRCULAR ECONOMY

CHARLES HAMPDEN-TURNER,
LINDA O'RIORDAN,
FONS TROMPENAARS

Published by
Filament Publishing Ltd
16, Croydon Road, Beddington, Croydon, Surrey CR0 4PA
+44(0)20 8688 2598
www.filamentpublishing.com

Capitalism in Crisis, Volume 1- Charles Hampden-Turner
ISBN 978-1-912635-56-6
© 2019 Charles Hampden-Turner

Printed by IngramSpark

Illustrator: David Lewis
www.davidlewiscartoons.com
davidlewiscartoons@gmail.com

TABLE OF CONTENTS

VOLUME 1 (THE CRISIS)

A Comedy of Errors
with potentially tragic consequences

To what extent should we convey ideas using words and text and to what degree should we rely on pictures and illustrations? Both Judeo-Protestant and Roman Catholic believers have come to blows on such issues and have smashed images. It is idolatrous to portray the divine save through words. "In the beginning was the Word…" and the printing press. In much of the West, the Word seems to have triumphed, yet in East Asia words themselves are picture-graphs and composites of ideas. In this book we have yielded much space to pictures and our audience are neither children nor artists but those who think.

The comic and comedy are widely regarded as flippant and unserious, aiming to entertain not inform. We seek to invoke the serious side of comedy, which is to laugh at yourself before it is too late. In Ancient Greece, comedy and tragedy were the two faces of their religion. The comic festival of Dionysus was held in December, the tragic festival in late April-May. It was said that if you could not laugh in December you would weep in May. The dramas were not entertainment, they were worship of the vagaries of the human condition. In comedy, opposed values bounce off each other unexpectedly and harmlessly and people who think themselves important are seen as absurd. In tragedy, opposed values grind painfully against each other and suffering is palpable. Comedy is "first aid" for human errors. Tragedy confronts you with the consequences. Yet because it is "play", it does not hurt so much and the audience learns from what they watch not to enact such folly. It is better to bounce than to grind. Let us learn to laugh while there is still time.

Introduction to Volume 1

In the first volume we investigate what has gone wrong. In Part I we state that wealth is created by all stakeholders working as one, that is employees, suppliers, customers the community, the government, the environment and the shareholders. There is a good reason why shareholders are put last; they can only collect what the other stakeholders have created between them. They are not last in importance – we need equality – they are last in time. What they earn depends on how well they have endowed those who do the actual work. Employees, suppliers and customers well served will produce better goods and more revenue. Shareholders must wait for this work to be done. Nations that treat their stakeholders well are growing apace. Stakeholder capitalism is the next evolutionary step.

Unfortunately, shareholders demand and have received priority over all other stakeholders and increase the share of wealth they receive by diminishing the shares received by others. When this happens, productivity and innovation flag. This situation has been likened to cancer in the human body in a book written by the founder of Whole Foods, John Mackey, published by Harvard Business School Press. It forms a vicious circle of shareholder dominance, exploiting both employees and the environment. It also leads to the disruptive crash of companies like Compaq who outsourced their core competences to rival companies who could do it cheaper, only to find themselves replaced by their own contractors. Companies increasingly buy back their own shares, which cause the prices to spike temporarily and allows those very few managers with share options to make a killing. It does nothing for the company itself and is a sterile manoeuvre akin to masturbation. Companies who treat their stakeholders best are actually in danger of a takeover – the fate of Cadbury's. The more spent on training, developing, R&D, suppliers, quality and helping customers, the more a raider can capture and offer exclusively to shareholders instead. Takeover targets are well, not poorly managed! Big companies increasingly buy up small creative companies, failing to grow themselves. Wall Street increasingly gains at the expense of Main Street, hence the simmering rage Trump has plugged into.

We next examine the effect of money on the development of industry. Is the purpose of industry to make money? Or is the purpose of money to make industry? America and the US supports the first and China supports the second which is self-evidently superior.

It is industry that gets things done. We show that contrary to common belief, money does not buy creativity and innovation. Those presented with a problem will solve it sooner and better without money being offered. The offer of cash incentives impedes solution. Pay for performance fails for similar reasons;

people concentrate on getting the money and neglect the problems. They fail to innovate because no money is attached to what superiors did not anticipate. They do the easier, better paid jobs and ignore challenges. Sales people on commission only are more likely to cheat and lie; after all no one cares for them, only the money they make! The cash nexus erodes innovation. None of this means that money has no uses but it should follow innovation, not precede it. Move the money to where the innovation is but do not expect it to elicit innovation in the first place.

Money by itself is sterile. No two coins ever created a third coin or ever will. Banks make money via leverage but this does not create wealth; it applies a magnifying glass to gains and to losses, hence the crash of 2008 and the need for tax payers to bail banks out.

All this results in gross inequality with past financial results pre-empting future learning goals and a Pandora's Box of social problems arising from being so unequal that your self-expression is extinguished. The values most favoured by women are submerged along with their earning power. The flaming tombstone of

Grenfell Tower is the symbol of a predatory capitalism that put money before the lives of poor people. Part of the problem is the discipline of Economics which, seeing man as a covetous machine, has lost the soul.

The problem with the "survival of the fittest" is that the unit of survival includes our environment and we will sink together. As for consuming more and more, obesity will soon kill as many as malnutrition. If the Chinese produce ever more and we consume ever more - the result is foregone.

We turn finally to the effect of money on the psyche and the influence of "the more, the better". Thinking in straight lines leads straight to excess, to single principle imperialism that wants either Brexit or its negation. The dream of unbridled power leads straight to blowing up the whole world with H-bombs three hundred times and imagining this makes us more strong and more secure. We want to be winners despite the losers this will spawn. We want to hurl our harpoons at the whale, Moby Dick, symbol of God's creation, and are surprised when he goes berserk with rage.

Trying to globalize by subjecting the whole world to our financial control leads to 9/11 and an attack on the World Trade Centre; overweening lawfulness triggers savage and merciless exceptionalism. We cannot control it all. We should not try. Trying to control the world through numbers does not work. It is blind to qualities, as the body count in Vietnam should have taught us. The whole notion of strategy assumes we want to beat people rather than serve them and that there exists somewhere an unbeatable combination like the conquests of Alexander the Great. What we get instead are wars of attrition with identical weapons on both sides leading to bloody stalemates.

Part II contrasts a wealth-creating cycle that generates surplus value with a wealth-destroying cycle that stagnates the economy and impoverishes us. The difference between the two is that in the first, investors generously support all other stakeholders, i.e. employees, suppliers, customers, the community, government, and the environment and then take a share of the wealth these created between them. Investors are stakeholders and depend on the productivity of those who are industrious. But we do not know how well these producers can do until they are fully funded and properly trained and developed. They must be given a chance to excel or we shall never know what they might have accomplished with more support. The bonds and relationships between shareholders and producers must stay intact.

In the wealth-destroying cycle these same relationships have been severed. Shareholders make sure they get their money by siphoning this off from other stakeholders. Wages are held down by threats of redundancies, jobs are outsourced to cheaper locations, training and R&D are cut, suppliers are paid late and forced to cut prices by threats of terminated contracts, customers receive less quality and poorer service, governments are denied tax receipts by passing money around the world or keeping it abroad, the environment is plundered and all these "savings" given to shareholders. No wonder employees become disengaged, growth slows and world market-shares shrink. Wages in the US have flat-lined for a generation or more. There is growing resentment among people who do not understand what is happening but are invited to blame Europe, Mexicans or foreigners in general. Note that the economy is circular whether successful or not, either a virtuous circle of a vicious one.

Part III considers wicked problems that never seem to go away but keep on cropping up over the decades and generations. This re-occurrence has its origins in persisting errors in how we conceive our social reality; so long as we think in particular ways the crises keep coming. The Achilles Heel in all these problems is anxiety and our means of controlling that anxiety which typically makes things worse. For example, our societies and our companies are growing increasingly diverse, yet engaging diverse people and dealing with them greatly raises anxiety and tension and we wish these foreigners would go away and stop making us tense. We desperately cling to racist dogmas to keep them away, while the more sophisticated invent codes of correctness which have a similar function and are formulaic. The tension between Diversity-Engagement leads to Brexit and walls along America's southern border with Mexico. But this is an echo of America's Aliens and Seditions Act of 1798. We blame those who make us anxious by turning free floating anxieties which we are helpless to counter and barely understand into fear of specific scapegoats whom we can punish, expel and persecute. My next child will not be still born if we burn the witch that cursed me.

Another wicked problem, that of alcoholism, affects the tension-relaxation of the human body, the sympathetic nervous system and the para-sympathetic system. People who are very manipulative raise their tension very high and cannot relax in love and friendship with others. They discover that alcohol is a relaxant and manipulate their own bodies into relaxing. Yet their bodies so crave relaxation, that after one drink they cannot stop. We seem obsessed with the desire to turn the social sciences into hard science and predict and control what others will do, which pits cause and effect against mutuality. If we "caused" other people to behave, we would no longer be free. The very attempt is ludicrous and doomed to revolt. We appear to be increasingly trapped between Right and Left on the political spectrum as

their positions reify into rocks of rectitude. On the right all problems are caused by deficient people not meeting standards. On the left all problems are caused by defective standards not meeting people.

We also seem doomed to lurch from boom to bust and from greed to fear. The market is subject to booms which we dare not slow lest we lose money, but which yield to panic when correction comes. The gap between work and welfare has become a gulf in which millions fall and subsist. Internet platforms sell data that undermines democracies. The anonymity offered by the internet severs the responsibility for what we say, from the freedom to say it. Management seems to have conquered labour whose purchasing power is now so low that managers and their companies suffer.

Part IV is called Mind-set, Re-set and is about how we can start to rethink and re-frame policies laid out in Volume 2. We must understand that the Industrial Age is giving way to the Age of Nature, with the life-sciences to the fore. We must learn to sustain what sustains us. We have to stop believing in the

Machine in the Sky or market mechanism, an absentee Protestant deity that rewards prudence and punishes sloth. It makes a poor object of worship. The economy is more like a tree or living system. Nature is circular, systemic, paradoxical and fractal. Societies construct their own realities and we must learn to re-construct and rid ourselves of wicked problems described earlier. That we are alive means that the whole is inevitably more than its parts. Our bodies are largely water. Values are like waves in water. Wealth is created from aesthetic patterns in these wholes. Nor do we have the power to command nervous systems not our own. They will lash back at us with unintended consequences. We seek mutuality freely exchanged and agreed among us.

Adam Smith was half right; self-interest spurs our willingness to serve others, but he missed the complementary insight, serving others is in our own self-interests. The two halves do not "cause" but trigger circularity, a helix of growth and development. We have to stop thinking of isolated events which bombard us and start to observe patterns, systems and the mental models which perpetuate errors. The basis of nature is paradoxical because science looks at how the human nervous system interacts with the external world. It examines the clash of our sense organs with whatever is "out there". If our brains have two distinct hemispheres, so will that which our brains receive; particles and waves, position and movement for example.

Were we to regard values as waves with frequencies then many of our bitter ideological disputes would cease. We need a "water logic", not the survival of the fittest but the survival of the finest fit. Nature itself is full of fractals, shapes that defy polarization and are both wholes and parts, both lawful and unique. What our social sciences try to do is impose order on a world full of varieties and exceptions. They seek to control us. The whole notion of the average person erodes the rich variety of our talents, as does the view of an elephant as a mere collection of familiar objects when in fact it is a living whole. We must save ourselves from the blind men of simplification. There is a larger whole just beyond the horizon if we keep searching. We end with the beginning, with the great funeral oration of Pericles that summed a legacy that was to enlighten the world. Can we get back to it?

WHAT YOU LEAVE BEHIND IS NOT WHAT IS ENGRAVED IN STONE MONUMENTS, BUT WHAT IS WOVEN INTO THE LIVES OF OTHERS.

PERICLES

PART 1:

THE CRISIS WE FACE

A) IT IS STAKEHOLDERS WHO ARE DOING THE ACTUAL WORK

SUSTAINABILITY REQUIRES THE EFFORTS OF ALL STAKEHOLDERS WORKING TOGETHER TO RESCUE THE PLANET.

Wealth can only be created and the planet saved by all those with a stake in organizations working together. It is simply absurd to claim that employees, suppliers, customers, and the environment are mere "agents" for shareholders, that someone who has owned shares for ten minutes "owns" the work of a 20-year employee or 40-year supplier, or cares about the planet. Sustainability will require employees, customers, government, and community and investors to cooperate. They must be allowed to "own" what they have helped to create. Wealth creation and a saved planet belong to all of us and depend on all of us giving what we can.

Shareholders are entitled to the residue after everyone else has received their fair share, but pushing to the front of the line is not waiting for the residue to appear, it is subordinating the interests of those you rely on to create wealth in the first place. It is not simply unjust but stupid. Ed Freeman first championed stakeholders when he was at SRI International in the eighties and has fought for the idea ever since. Many emerging nations to whom existing technologies are transferred find they hardly need shareholders at all! The cost of this capital is high and the Asian financial crisis of 1997 was largely triggered by sudden panic among Western equity markets. Sovereign Wealth Funds have now replaced these as a source on which stakeholders can rely. Much of the rivalry in Southeast Asia comes from family companies with a service ethic towards their societies who think long-term and want their companies to support grandchildren.

RELATIONSHIPS AMONG STAKEHOLDERS ARE THE KEYS TO WEALTH CREATION

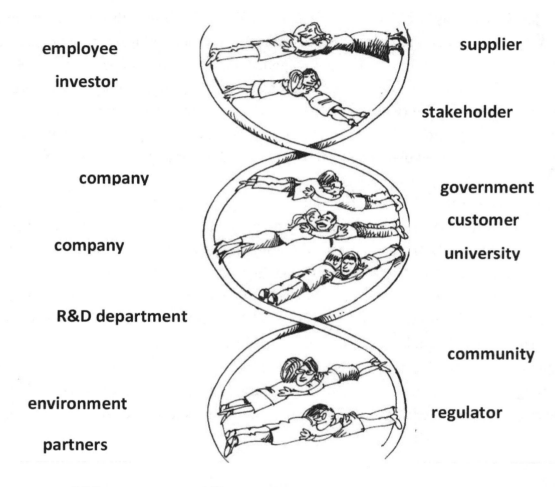

employee

investor

company

company

R&D department

environment

partners

supplier

stakeholder

government

customer

university

community

regulator

WHAT THE CHINESE CALL GUANXI IS THEIR STRONGEST BUSINESS VALUE AND SPEAKS OF THE INTIMATE RELATIONS BETWEEN PEOPLE AND THEIR VALUES.

What creates wealth are not so much particular persons, as the quality of relationships among these. Companies grow where these are in harmony. A problem with shareholder domination which we have been examining is that a company, its suppliers, its partners and its customers may consist of scores or even hundreds of different companies and their shareholders, all trying to maximize their own returns.

This does not make for an industrial eco-system of cooperation but an extended conflict among rival entities with the larger companies taking the lion's share from smaller companies and making sure that they survive, but learn their place in the pecking order. Suppliers are run against each other and the lowest bid demanded. Suppliers are paid late to remind them of their chronic dependence.

Relationships are not nurturant but adversarial. An innovative break-through is not communicated to the customer but used to win a bidding war. The opportunity to cut costs by mutual adjustments, to fate-share and to gain-share, or to invest in one another is forgone. The environment is not our enemy but something with which we engage beneficially. The habit of looking at units themselves, rather than at how well units relate to each other, dies hard. Accountants cannot measure it so "it does not count". Yet in a world full of knowledge, it is eco-systems which compete with eco-systems. Rather than competing with those we encounter day by day, we need to cooperate and forge win-win solutions with them. Instead of cursing government and regulation we can make sure it is fair and gives our company the advantage it deserves.

STAKEHOLDER CAPITALISM IS OVERTAKING SHAREHOLDER CAPITALISM

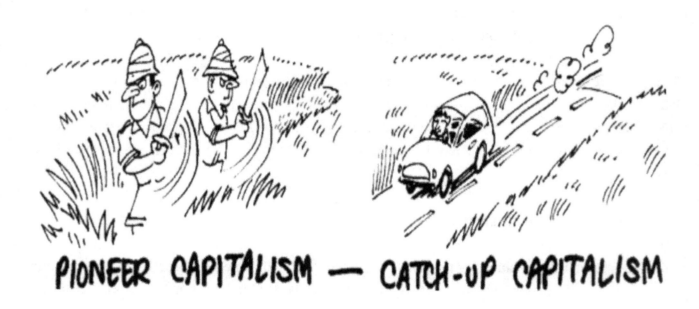

PIONEER CAPITALISM — CATCH-UP CAPITALISM

THERE ARE TWO FORMS OF CAPITALISM IN THE WORLD,

There are two forms of capitalism in the world, the kind which pioneered capitalism in the first place and the kind that enabled nations to come from behind and catch-up. Nations that took off economically in the first wave, largely but not entirely the Anglo-sphere, North America, UK, Australia and New Zealand, must be distinguished from the second wave, France, Germany, Scandinavia and from the third wave, Japan, the Pacific Rim, China and India. We refer to fast followers as the second and third waves. The different waves experienced very different challenges and circumstances.

Pioneer capitalism differs from the second and third waves in the following respects. The pioneers grow slowly having to cut through the elephant grass to build a road. Even in the industrial revolution growth was slow by modern standards, although the whole phenomenon of growth was at that time new to the world. The catch-up capitalists grow much faster since the road and the car had now been built and they had only to use these transferred technologies. No nation had grown faster or longer than Japan from 1950-1990, just as no nation has grown faster and longer than China, from 1980 to this time. They also differ markedly in their use of equity capital from shareholders and their insistence that shareholders are sovereign over the whole company. This insistence is largely confined to the Anglo-sphere. East Asians use the Japanese model of capitalism that gives shareholders very limited powers. When Alibaba launched on Wall Street, the largest IPO in the world to that date, it emphasised that employees came first, customers second and shareholders brought up the rear. This did not stop shareholders subscribing! Germany, which caught up Britain three times, used a network of provincial banks to make long-term, low interest loans at a much lower cost of capital. Using shareholders is expensive! They are not necessary to catch-up capitalists whose risks are much smaller than that of pioneers. Pioneer capitalists tend to champion entrepreneurship, individualism, de-regulation and private gain for shareholders, while catch-up capitalist tend to champion rapid social learning, a mobilized community, government sponsorship and public benefit for all stakeholders. Brexit has much to do with these clashing values. Have we over-learned a once winning combination?

STAKEHOLDER CAPITALISM IS REPLACING SHAREHOLDER DOMINANCE

THE BEST KIND OF CAPITALISM DRAWS ON THE COMMITMENTS OF ALL WITH A STAKE.

Stakeholder capitalism is winning across the globe. China is the chief exponent of stakeholder capitalism. It has a stock market, notably in Shanghai, but few take it seriously. You have to be consistently profitable over a number of years to be listed on it, so that platform companies like Alibaba had to turn to Wall Street for their IPO. Shareholders are needed to launch pioneer industries but if you are fast-following the risks are much lower. Besides, saving rates in East Asia are traditionally much higher so there is a great deal of cheap capital available. The world is not short of capital; it sloshes around the globe like an over-filled bath-tub. However, the world IS short of human skills and inventiveness which is where stakeholders come in. Fast growing economies are growing the skills of their people. Slow growing economies are pleasing plutocrats and favouring fat-cats. In any cost-competition, as is occurring among supermarkets, private companies like Aldi and Lidl can cut back on profits for the family in exchange for larger market shares. After all, they are thinking of preserving the companies for their grandchildren. Public companies like Tesco have to squirrel away hefty junks for shareholders who will desert them in droves were the price to fall. They must keep paying shareholders and activist investors will hold them to the mark and attempt a take-over if they do not. Growing and training your people and your suppliers takes time, but increasingly, public companies do have that time. Shares turn over too fast. The share-holder wants his money in weeks not years and cares not a fig for the actual company, only for what it pays. The evolution of capitalism has reached a new stage. Sovereign wealth funds are the new kinds of responsible investor, for example, making sure Kraft did not acquire Unilever and siphon off training funds.

B) Shareholder dominance: is it cancerous?

If you expand unilaterally any one element in a system, you will first unbalance, then destroy it.

Is it not outrageous to state that the threat posed by shareholders to public companies is analogous to cancer's threat to the human body? Only an anarchist or closet Marxist could issue such a challenge. As for publishing such a claim, that is nearly as bad. Except that the accusation comes from John Mackey, founder and head of Whole Foods, the $12 billion-dollar chain, and published by Harvard Business School Press in the book *Conscious Capitalism*. A better question might be "When are we going to wake up to this tragedy?" Numerous articles have made the same point and Jack Welch at his retirement from GE, the world's largest high-tech manufacturer, called maximizing shareholder wealth "the dumbest idea in the world". He should know, he did it for thirty years! But there is no mistaking the words of Mackey and his co-author, Professor Raj Sisodia. "We find that cancer is a useful metaphor for what is wrong with stakeholders in many businesses. The human body has over 100 million cells, interacting cooperatively with each other to stay alive, grow and reproduce. Cancer is a breakdown of the harmonious interdependence among cells that is essential to good health. A cancerous tumour starts to grow because some cells start to divide and grow, ignoring the warning signs from the body's immune system; eventually killing its host (and itself as well, cancer is ultimately suicidal)." Share prices have reached an all-time high in the USA. Are the rest of us as fortunate? The point is NOT that shareholders should receive less. We and other pensioners would like them to receive more. But they will only enlarge the whole pie if they stop putting themselves first. The current short-termism is fatal. Quick, riskless money-making is a fraud. Maximise any one element in a system and disaster will ensue. It will wreck the equilibrium of the whole.

THE VICIOUS CIRCLE OF SHAREHOLDER DOMINANCE

WHAT HAPPENS WHEN SHAREHOLDERS GRAB THE LION'S SHARE

The vicious circle of shareholder dominance starts with corporations competing for equity investment at the top of the illustration. If shareholders believe they can get a better deal elsewhere they will sell their shares and the company's available resources will shrink. The danger is that it will be worth more dead than alive and their resources will be sold off and their human resources declared redundant. In order to make as much for shareholders as possible, wages are shaken from the pockets of employees and suppliers are squeezed on price. Investments in Research and Development are cut back, as is training and human development. The corporation helps itself to nature's bounty and dumps its waste and welfare costs on the socio-political environment and avoids taxes. When the industrial eco-system starts to wilt and to under-perform, shareholders demand even MORE rather than less and the circle becomes more vicious still. The pathology is self-perpetuating. There is a systematic transfer of resources to shareholders, away from other stakeholders which has accelerated over the years. These are not investors, they are traders who hold their shares for a matter of weeks. Why would we expect them to care? All this is the legacy of the Reagan-Thatcher era, when public companies began to under-perform, a trend increasing of late.

DISRUPTIVE INNOVATION AND HOLLOWING OUT THE CORPORATION

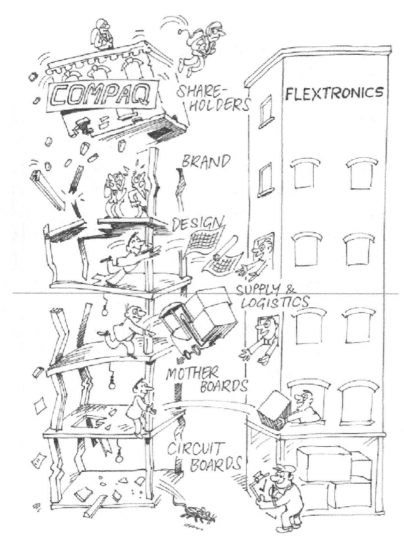

HOW TO PROFIT AS YOU GIVE AWAY THE STORE.

We recently pointed a film camera at Clayton Christensen of Harvard, and he gave us this illustration of his study of disruptive innovation. "It is the pursuit of profit that is the causal mechanism behind both prosperity and failure. Disruption can occur when a company comes in right at the bottom of the market in the least demanding sector, as Toyota did, and then moves up tier by tier...at the very lowest tier of the value chain, it then integrates forward." There is an interesting illustration in the interaction between Singapore-based Flextronics and its Texan customer Compaq. Flextronics started by making the simplest of circuit boards inside Compaq computers. It then asked "Why don't you let us make your motherboards as well? We can do it for 20% less cost." Compaq analysts looked at the issue and said "Gosh they could! If we gave them all the circuit-making manufacturing we could get this off our balance sheet." So they shovelled that over ...revenues were unaffected and their profits really improved...It made sense for one to get in and the other to get out. Then Flextronics came back... "You shouldn't be bothered with Assembly. We can do it for 20% less." So Compaq moved that over. Flextronics came back again. "You should not be bothered by the supply chain and logistics. Most of it is in this part of the world anyway (Singapore). It's not your core competence. We can do it for 20% less." Again, Compaq's revenues were unaffected but their profits improved. Their return on assets was better because they had almost no assets left and Wall Street loves asset-light companies! They were into value-added services and Wall Street loves those too. Flextronics came back again. "You should not have to design your computer. It's only component selection and we handle your components anyway. Your strength is your brand." Flextronics came back once more but not to Compaq this time but to Best Buy. "We can give you this brand, that brand or any brand for 20% less!" Bingo! One has arrived and the other has gone. Compaq hollowed itself out storey by storey for added profit and collapsed.

IS BUYING BACK YOUR OWN SHARES A FORM OF STERILITY?

A RATHER DERISORY SUBSTITUTE FOR PRO-CREATION.

We have slightly changed Woody Allen's quip from his film *Annie Hall*. The original line was "Don't knock masturbation; is it is sex with someone I really love." But, joking aside, we need to ask whether a company buying back its own shares is doing more than stimulating itself. Certainly, the act is without consequence in generating wealth or offspring. No customer is engaged. The act is one of sterility. A reason sometimes advanced is that it gives a company more control over its destiny. Fewer external shareholders means fewer people objecting to what management wants to do. But this fails to convince. "Activist" shareholders, those most likely to give top managers trouble, are unlikely to sell their shares for small gains. What buy-backs do is create an all-too-brief spike in the price of shares because of the additional demand, which allows those who knew it was coming to exercise their share options and sell these at a gain. The money comes from other shareholders not in the know and is akin to insider trading. No notice of share buy-backs need be given so this is done surreptitiously, another similarity to masturbation. General Motors bought back their shares twenty times before going bankrupt and flying up to Washington in their corporate jet to ask for a bail-out. It is also the epitome of short-termism since the share-price gain has nothing to do with being more productive or successful. It only became common about twenty years ago and Hillary Clinton had promised to end the practice in the event of winning the election for President. It raises the share price while doing nothing to improve the performance of the actual company. We find it hard to be censorious but nor are we in the least impressed. It is one more of the excesses of individualism, of using companies for our own pleasure, not building them up to serve future generations. Engaging someone else is not only more enjoyable but more vital.

WHY STAKEHOLDER COMPANIES ARE MORE LIKELY TO BE RAIDED

The official rationale for shareholder power is that they can remove incompetent managers, but this stumbles over the repeated finding that those companies most likely to be raided are those who are well, rather than badly managed, and who are out-performing their peers. The more generous a company is in training, developing and educating its employees, its suppliers and its customers, and the more assiduously it pays its taxes to governments and reduces its emissions, the more likely it is to attract a hostile takeover bid. Why is this? Because all such activities have immediate costs and longer-term pay-offs. You can cut the costs and give these straight to shareholders, most of whom will be long gone by the time the investments in people and the environment pay off. Kraft made a bid for Cadbury's, a venerable Quaker company, often cited by human resource experts for its personnel policies and its culture of learning. They undertook to close none of its plants but promptly reneged on that promise. Kraft later took over Heinz and made 15,000 employees redundant giving the saving in salaries to shareholders. Kraft-Heinz (see the crocodile in the illustration opposite) then spoke of making a bid for Unilever, a much larger company. It would have had to take on debt and saddle Unilever with this, so that its shareholders were being offered their own future dividends. Paul Polman, CEO of Unilever, refused to discuss the issue and Kraft-Heinz withdrew its bid rather than make a hostile one. One source of Unilever's strength was that 75% of its shareholders support its long-term orientation and its investment in people, especially its public health campaigns in India and Africa around hand washing and access to clean water. Its policies are supported by Sovereign Wealth Funds in Norway, China, Singapore, Sweden and others. It helps, educates and advises more than 200,000 women world-wide and demands that its suppliers support human rights. Its Dove campaign to raise the self-esteem of adolescent women has over 2 million members. Many of its disinfectant and cleaning brands are life-saving. We recommend organized resistance to predators like Kraft-Heinz.

ACQUIRING AND TAKING OVER SMALL COMPANIES RATHER THAN LEARNING AND GROWING ONESELF

Companies like Pfizer to less and less of their own R&D and instead, buy up small creative companies

...yet the attempt to acquire the genius of others ends up as innovation pinned down, objectified, dead

TRYING TO BUY THE GENIUS OF ANOTHER GROUP OF PEOPLE

What happens when finance gets control of everything, is that public companies cease to research, innovate and grow organically, via the development of their own people and their use of scientific knowledge. Instead they try to acquire these qualities by buying up small and medium sized companies. But is it possible to "own" and "possess" the genius of another group or culture? How would the money-men appreciate what they had acquired or see in it more than a temporary stream of income? The metamorphosis from a hungry caterpillar to a beautiful butterfly and pollinator is something very strange and precious, as is the capacity to create value and substance from ideas and imaginations. We strongly suspect that this cannot be priced, understood or acquired, much less in the language of accountancy. It is small companies that create most jobs, grow fastest, evoke most passion and are frail and often short-lived. Catching them, collecting them and keeping them as trophies, does an economy scarce favours. We need to listen to our creators, not colonize them, to encounter them as equals and learn from them. Note the broken rope or disconnect at the centre of the illustration. Money does not grasp the significance of pharmacology, chemistry, antibodies or healing. These have their own logics. We need more small, creative companies. When they are captured they are pinned down and mostly die. The bureaucratic culture of a large company kills and crushes that of smaller ones. As the spirit within the larger public corporation atrophies, its appetite for the spark it lacks only grows, hence the hunger is unappeasable, the circle is vicious.

WALL STREET VS. MAIN STREET: IS FINANCE CONSTRICTING INDUSTRY?

Wall Street & the Financial sector

Wealth creating sector

WEALTH-CREATION HAS THE LIFE SQUEEZED OUT OF IT

This looks into the issue of whether the expansion of the financial sector of the economy helps or hinders the industrial sector. Does Wall Street serve Main Street or does it help itself, perhaps at the expense of Main Street? Banks are not prima face contributors to the economy but rather distributors of the currency needed to conduct business. They supply liquidity without which it would be impossible for businesses to function. No one suggests we could do without banks. They certainly make money, in part because they lend out money greatly in excess of their own assets. But this is not to say they create wealth. Our test of wealth creation asks whether the parties to a transaction have more money than they began with; since banks charge interest on loans, they get more money but their borrowers pay for this by keeping less. What borrowers do with the money is produce something customers will buy and here wealth is created. The bank facilitates this process but no wealth is generated by the bank itself or its contracts with customers.

There are two disturbing bodies of research which looked at several Western economies and found that rapid expansion of the financial sector was accompanied by reductions in the industrial sector. Why might this happen? Because the banks are keeping more of the money that passes through their hands and less of this ends up with contributors to the economy. Because banks tend to pay higher salaries than industry and so cream off much of the talent. Then there is the fact that the financial sector has an interest in maximizing shareholders' incomes and helps them extract as much money from industry as possible, leaving them less to invest in R&D, training, skills development and growth. Middle and working-class salaries have been flat-lining for some years while the income of banks and the financial sector has climbed. Historically we have been here before. It was Wall Street that built up the giant trusts at the end of 19th century which the Sherman Antitrust Act fought and constrained. These were nation-wide monopolies designed to impose prices.

❧

c) STAKEHOLDERS & INDUSTRY ARE A MERE MEANS TO ENRICHING OWNERS

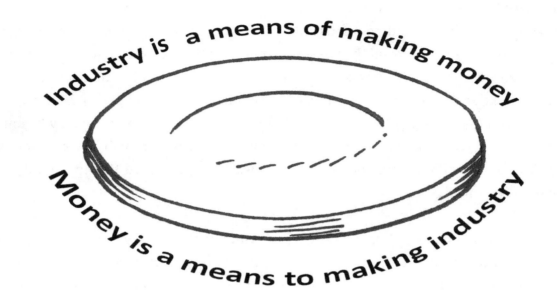

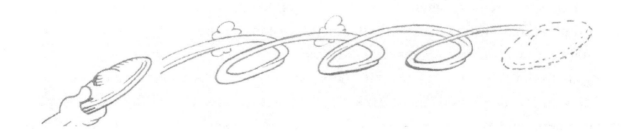

THE LOGIC OF WEALTH CREATION IS A CIRCLE, NOT A LINE.

At the top of the picture is the current idea that the prime purpose of industry is as a means to make money; in short, that money is the main objective. We should wring as much personal gain for shareholders from our industries as we can. Yet a moment's reflection should tell us that industry and leading a life that is industrious and productive is equally important, perhaps even more so, than is garnering as much as we can from this process. It is obvious that if we take too much money out of industry and do not put enough back in, then industry will begin to wilt. Wall Street will prefer financial fixes to the sustained work of building industry. In short, industry is an end in itself influencing the characters of people. It makes as much sense to say that money is means to making us industrious, that it finances wealth creation and the rate of economic development by which China is rising and much of the West falling. We will see in this section that money incentives actually reduce creative problem solving, that pay-for-performance has a dismal record, routinely denied, that bonus payments are a dangerously crude form of communication, that the scandal of the UK's Payment Protection Insurance (PPI) can be traced to the conscious manipulation of people through money incentives, that purely financial exchanges are sterile, that coins do not of themselves co-create. We will see that income inequalities within nations constitute a veritable Pandora's Box of social ills, and that the greater the disparity, the wider the cloud of social ills. We shall see that selfishness is busy eliminating social man.

Do money rewards kill creative problem-solving?

Money distracts us from solving problems.

People are motivated solely by money in all matters of economic exchange. Those with money can buy anything and almost everyone they want. All other motives and moods are secondary, right? Wrong, as it happens. Economics has missed perhaps the most significant value of them all, the urge to create and innovate, crucial to a developed economy. In the famous Candle Problem, two teams must solve a problem that requires a modicum of creativity. They must affix a lighted candle to the wall using just those elements displayed opposite. To do this it is necessary to use the box in which the thumb tacks came. It is not just a container. The box is tacked to the wall and the base of the candle anchored by another tack, pushed through the box. One team, on the left, is offered money to do this quickly and can see their reward. The other is offered no money but is told it will be timed for experimental purposes. The experiment has been repeated many times in many nations, rich and poor; even a month's wages for five minutes' work does not improve the performance of the incentivised team. Experiments dispensing with candles have also been tried but the results are very similar. The team offered rewards takes longer by some margin. Daniel Pink laid all this out in an address to the Royal Society for the Arts and in a TED talk. He and we conclude that paying people extra for solving a problem distracts their attention from the problem itself. They focus on the money and what the paymaster wants. The only way to get the incentivised team even close to winning is to take the tacks out of the box. This eliminates all complexity and the solution is simple, just the kind of jobs being automated and eliminated. When it comes to the prime purpose of our lives, economics misses the ball. All those fat bonuses and extravagant bribes are making us duller and more mediocre.

❧

WHY PAY-FOR-PERFORMANCE FAILS AGAIN AND AGAIN

THE JACKASS FALLACY

Harry Levinson, the Harvard professor, had the cartoon opposite drawn for him and called it the Jackass Fallacy. The idea of manipulating employees by money rewards is an open insult. It is not how human beings are. Not only did America grow much faster in the three decades after World War II when incentives were much lower, but rates of economic growth are much higher in China than in the USA, with a fraction of the incentives. But it was Alfie Kohn who pointed to the research results which clearly show what goes wrong. It robs tasks of their meaning. Children given money for fastening seat belts stop doing so when the money stops! Blood donated because the person was paid is more often contaminated. Pay-for-Performance (P-for-P) rewards people receiving help at the expense of those giving help. It wrongly assumes that the individual is solely responsible for output. It assumes that those in authority know just how valuable each job is, but they rarely do. What about innovation? There is no price affixed to what surprises people. What about problem-solving? People avoid problems which could lower their performance. P-for-P rewards conformity as opposed to originality. Employees "game the system" by seizing easy jobs that are known to be overpaid. P-for-P increases inequality because the bosses can claw back money for jobs not done to their satisfaction. It leads to resisting new technology because "performance" must be redefined. It leads to fellow workers punishing those who work "too hard" and raise managers' expectations. Industry has widely abandoned piece-work incentives in favour of quality circles. P-for-P lends itself to divide and rule tactics in the work-place, paying for compliance and punishing self-assertion. Despite hundreds of studies, the elite refuses to believe that their money cannot rule everyone and that by making more money they will have more power. They are addicted.

WHY THE BONUS CULTURE IS TOO CRUDE/ SIMPLISTIC TO WORK EFFECTIVELY

THE DEATH OF SUBTLE COMMUNICATION

The task of supervising the work of a subordinate is a very subtle and nuanced process. You have to express two contrasting values at the same time. You must SUPPORT the person so they continue their efforts and go on trying. You must CRITIQUE that person's performance so that they realize they must strive to do better and correct any mistakes. If the woman opposite believes you are on her side, that you back her career, value her as an employee, then she is likely to try even harder to perform superlatively. This is especially important where her work is creative, because creative efforts are rarely right the first time and must be refined and improved, part inspiration, part perspiration. The problem with bonuses is that they are too blunt, too crude, too black and white and their subtlety is zero. They fail entirely to communicate that you value that person but seek to improve her work. She has probably anticipated a bonus and booked a family vacation on the strength of it. When it is withheld it feels like a slap in the face. "Your work is not yet quite good enough" has been rendered as "You and your work are rejected". She is likely to leave at the first opportunity, so that her boss may give her the bonus simply to avoid the time and expense of hiring someone else! But he has now lost the critical side of his message. The more focused she is externally on her bonus, the less focused she is internally on what is true, beautiful, creative and self-fulfilling and of lasting value to humanity. The bonus culture has produced a harvest of predatory conduct, of pushing products on people because you are incentivized to do so and not because these are needed. The customer exists to make money for you. If you want your employees to beat up on the customer, you need to bribe them. Those selling PPI were mostly on commission only. Every customer they strong-armed produced a pay-off for them.

The UK's Payment Protection Insurance scandal

EMPLOYEES' TREATMENT IS PASSED ON TO CUSTOMERS

RELATING TO ONE ANOTHER'S INTEGRITY

EMPLOYER, EMPLOYEE AND CUSTOMER ARE MERELY MEANS TO AN END

THOSE MANIPULATED MANIPULATE CUSTOMERS IN TURN.

Payment Protection Insurance (PPI) was sold to bank customers in the UK on a very large scale. Million-pound fines were imposed on prominent lenders and they are still repaying customers for mis-selling from many years past. PPI was added to loans, mortgages and credit cards and ostensibly insured the borrower against bad loans, being fired, and the death or disablement of creditors. It added as much 16-25% to the cost of borrowing and was sold to some people who did not want it, did not need it and even some ineligible to claim. It was sold mostly by telephone sales by people on commission only. The idea that people work largely for money and personal gain succeeds in poisoning the whole system. Opposite we see the "clever" boss dangling the prospect of a bonus or incentive in front of a salesman. The more he sells, the more he will get. The boss is not interested in him as a person but in what he does for the company, his sales record. It is hardly surprising that the salesman passes on to the customer the way he has himself been treated. The customer, like the salesman, is a mere means to the end being sought by the company. Whether she needs or wants it is irrelevant. (40% of customers were unaware they had even bought it!). She is "motivated" to buy, by hints that her loan request may be turned down otherwise. The Citizens' Advice Bureau referred to it as a protection racket. Most of those selling PPI were on commission only, sometimes as high as 40%. To get sales people to be that ruthless you have to manipulate them. No one cares a damn for the actual sales person, only for what they make, so they end up not caring a damn for the market to whom they sell. They receive nothing at all unless they can con the customer. In this whole rigmarole, everyone tricks everyone and no one relates face-to-face to the another's integrity, see top right.

NO TWO COINS EVER CREATED A THIRD COIN OR EVER WILL

MONEY BY ITSELF IS STERILE.

Despite excitable books about the "alchemy of finance" and the ability to make vast amounts of money from money, the bald fact is that money by itself is sterile as far as wealth and value creation are concerned. No two coins co-habiting have ever produced a third coin and they never will. This does not mean that finance is useless or that bankers are villains. Although you can create money by leveraging, lending out more assets than you have and charging interest, this does not create wealth, as opposed to making money. Wealth is created when all parties to an enterprise have more resources between them than they began with. This happens when money borrowed from a bank is transformed into raw materials and components, which in turn are transformed into finished products. The whole thus formed may be very much more valuable than the sum of its parts, in the way that a house is more valuable than the bricks, wood, frames and tiles that went into it. When the house is sold and transformed back into money this surplus constitutes wealth, more than the parties began with. It follows that banks contribute to wealth creation when they serve industry, but not when they trade and speculate with each other or play in a world casino. This explains why the very big financial centres in the City and Wall Street may not assist Main Street at all and why the vast expansion of financial activity has been found to depress the larger economy. Pure finance is a zero-sum game with the larger players using other people's money to beat the smaller by betting enough to skew the odds in their favour. The size of their wagers raises prices enabling them to sell and make profits, benefitting only themselves.

WE HAVE TO BE MORE THAN BAR-CODES

DO CODES LOSE TOUCH WITH WHAT THEY CODIFY?

It is true that we live by buying and selling to each other and that what we work at and purchase says much about us, but this is no excuse for rendering our humanity as a barcode. This way of thinking chops and slices us into so many dead pieces. Our value to our society lies in what we purchase. We are in danger of becoming great jumbled heaps of groceries and possessions. Sellers see us as so many targets at which to take aim. True humanity lies rather in how these products are used, their relationships to our health and fitness, the relationships within the systems they comprise, whether or not they enhance our vitality and our full expression, whether and what they enable us to learn and develop our minds. Behind every new product there is a creative process and that is where true value lies in the powers of human expression, like the graceful dive of the woman depicted opposite. Products are not important in themselves, as things cluttering homes and attics, but they are important in the human capacities they unleash, the bodies they nourish, the life-styles they shape and the experiences they constitute. Even advertisers would be much wiser to consider what products mean to us. How does this company treat its female employees? What is its impact on the environment? Does it make the world a better place? Does it pay wages that enable people to live properly and, if not, why is it not training them to be of value? A product is more than a thing - it is an expression of the culture of the work place that made it and it is to these cultures that we should relate, buying that which enhances the human condition. The relationship of buyer and seller is one of mutual benefit. Is the buyer better off and if so by how much? There is nothing wrong or villainous about barcodes. They are useful in tracking the flow of goods. What is wrong is the shrinking of our perception and what we leave out of the equation. Life is not a pile of objects, but a process of weaving many elements together. Those who sell should be helping to develop us and live our lives more fully.

LEVERAGE AS THE GREAT TEMPTATION

SPECULATING WITH OTHER PEOPLE'S MONEY.

Many people speak of the "financial industry" and see it as competing with all other industries, competing well in the case of Wall Street and the City of London and not so well in other cases, like the Shanghai Stock Exchange. But is it just an industry like others? Is finance a contributor to the economy or a distributor of the counters with which all industries must play and use for their transactions? What happens when more and more of the money finance distributes sticks to its fingers as it passes through? In such an event the money made by the financial industry is like a tax on all other industries. An interesting case is bank leverage, a major way of making money for the bank but not a way of creating wealth for non-financial industries or society. What leverage means is that you can charge interest on money deposited and/or saved with you by customers. You can lend out much more money than you own (assets) and much more than is in your accounts and belongs to others banking with you. Leverage ratios go up and down but in the months before the crash of 2008 were as much as thirty times higher than what was held by banks. This led to the joke "I have bad news and good news – we have lost a lot of money but little of it is ours."

Banks take high risks with people's money. What they are betting on is that most customers will not demand their money back at the same time and usually this is true but not always. While banks make money steadily in normal times, when they lose money the lose thirty times as much, as leverage goes into reverse. They are then wiped out to the tune of $5 trillion and we, the public, must bail them out and suffer years of austerity and squeezed incomes. Donald Trump is the symptom of public indignation with this system. "Moral hazard" occurs when banks know they will win in good times and be rescued in bad times and that the money they play with is not theirs. They gain from the risks their customers have no choice but to make. "Heads I win... tails you lose."

❦

D) Gross Inequality - the Social Cost

FINANCIAL RESULTS ARE ALL THERE IS TO IT. LEARNING BE DAMNED.

While finance is of course essential to the proper conduct of business, it can have its importance exaggerated. A great deal of the confidence, assurance and precision finance brings to us, comes from the fact that it is historical and faces to the past. The profit made today may have its origins in events long-gone and resources no longer present. Moreover, the world is changing at an ever-faster rate. The crucial question becomes how are we to learn about the future and stay in touch with new realities? Future learning goals on the left of the picture opposite rarely get as much attention compared to the bottom line. They are too vague, too ambiguous, too elusive. The purpose of business is to enrich its investors, not to provide a free education to its employees and suppliers! And yet, unless employees learn at an ever-faster pace how to engage their changing environments, they can generate none of the resources needed to repay investors. They need information, ever more of it. They need to learn faster than employees of rival companies. You cannot exploit your competitive position in the future unless you have explored enough to gain that position here and now. Making good profits can actively mislead us unless we have invested in discovery, innovation and future goals. What we learn today may not pay off for five years or more but unless we learn it we are doomed. And the longer run comes home to us each and every day. Dr Robert Kaplan and Dr David Norton have written of the Balanced Scorecard. We need to measure financial results and have auditors sign-off on these, so corporate cultures give considerable importance to the figures of quarterly profits. But do they give equal stress to the learning, creativity and innovation needed to produce these profits initially and why do companies that have been profiting for decades that dominate their industries suddenly crash? As Professor Michael Tushman at Harvard has put it, they have exploited too much and have explored too little. The scores do not just need to be balanced but to be aligned, so that profits of the last quarter are spent on future learning goals.

⚘

THE PESTILENCE RAVAGING WHOLE SOCIETIES.

In the Greek myth, Pandora disobeyed warnings and opened her golden box, from which escaped scores of human afflictions which have haunted us ever since. In our present age that box is labelled INEQUALITY, not absolute inequality, but relative inequality within nations. As Richard Wilkinson and Kate Pickett have shown in their book *The Spirit Level,* there is no difference in human welfare among nations whose citizens earn $20,000 a year and up. Earning twice this makes no difference. It is the disparity within countries and between citizens that does the harm. Among the most equal of the 24 richest countries are Japan, Norway, Finland, Sweden, Belgium and Austria. Among the most unequal are the USA (by a long way), UK, Portugal, Australia, New Zealand and Israel. The USA is roughly as wealthy as Norway but has sixteen times as many of its citizens incarcerated. Inequality keeps very bad company. Unequal nations have more homicide, more violence, more alcoholism and addiction, more severe punishments, poorer child welfare, more obesity, lower maths and literacy scores, higher drop-out rates, more single mothers and still births, worse mental health, more suicide, less upward mobility and lower aspirations. No matter how noble your cause, whether it is Oxfam volunteers or teaching nuns, inequality corrupts. Why is equality so important? Because it is the process by which we engage each other. There is no greater respect that treating others as our equals. To defer is to doubt your fitness to judge. A coaching relationship is among the most equal of all relationships.

THE CONSEQUENCES OF WOMEN EARNING LESS

BEHIND EVERY INJUSTICE IS THE THREAT OF FORCE.

The figures opposite come from *The Sunday Times* of April 8th 2018 and are for the United Kingdom. They clearly show that inequality towards women is a function of inequality in general and has to do with the unequal treatment of the values which women personify. If you discriminate against women you thereby detract from what women value and you subordinate perspectives we need to create wealth. We know quite a lot about what female managers prefer as contrasted to men. Women play roles complementary to men so as to better love and sustain them. Relationships require us to provide what is missing. Men are more oriented to rules of universal applicability and women more oriented to particular exceptions, but of course rules need exceptions if they are to improve. Men are more individualistic, women more concerned with social units, especially the family. Yet we need the second to support the first. Men are more neutral in their expression of emotions, women more passionate, yet we need much more passionate engagement in in our work if we are to create, innovate and serve. Men are more analytical, atomistic and specific, women more synthesizing, holistic and diffuse in the way they think, yet everything taken apart has to be put together again. Men prefer tasks to relationships yet tasks need to be related. One of the quickest ways of catching up Southeast Asia may be to empower Western women, since they have the characteristics of East Asian management in general and the same saving insights.

THE FIERY TOMBSTONE OF OUR PREDATORY CAPITALISM

"HAD WE BUT LISTENED AND LEARNED..."

A moment of truth came with the seventy-two lives lost in Grenfell Tower fire in North Kensington in London on June 14, 2017. It revealed in the starkest terms how very little the Royal Borough of Chelsea and Kensington, one of the richest in Europe, cared for its own poor tenants. Even after the fire, it could barely speak to them. Informally, the spontaneous community response was magnificent, while the formal response had shamed officials who were hiding. There was a single spiral staircase for leaving the building, soon full of smoke and expiring bodies. The fatal instructions issued were to stay put so that the compliant all died. The cladding used to make the building more attractive to the eye was made of combustible material because this was cheaper and there were no sprinklers or workable fire-doors for the same reason. The only firemen's ladders available reached to the 11th floor of 23 floors. Stacking the poor vertically on top of each other is the most economic use of expensive land. The fast combustion of cladding was known from previous fires and the protest of the Tenants Action Group and its prediction of fatal fire had been ignored. While £11.8 billion had been budgeted only £8.6 billion was spent. Sprinklers would have cost £200,000. Non-flammable cladding would has cost £2 more per panel. It was a nice little earner. The borough spent £39.8 million and collected £55 million from some of the poorest in the land. The grim, charred skeleton stands in silent reproach. As a spokesman put it, "Had we been listened to and respected, Grenfell Tower would not have happened. It was as simple as that." It is a monument to lost relationships and the loss of humanity in our, now predatory, capitalism.

Economics has lost the soul of mankind

"It could be shown...that it was advantageous to roll students into pellets, flatten them into cakes and stretch them into cables..."

Valuable possessed by the valiant

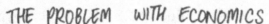

THE PROBLEM WITH ECONOMICS

CURRENT PRINCIPLES OF ECONOMIC SCIENCE & CALCULATION

PELLETS, CAKES AND CABLES

A SCIENCE WORTHY OF THE FULLNESS OF HUMAN ENDOWMENT WHICH RECOGNISES THE SOUL IN MAN

RE-INSERTION ATTENDED BY VARIOUS INCONVENIENCES

THE LIVING PERSON'S SOUL, PASSION & MORAL IMPULSE

John Ruskin wrote his famous essay *Unto This Last* about the failure of economics to include the creative spirit in people, but rather treating them as "covetous machines". Purchased objects have no value apart from the individual's purpose in using them. A man in a shipwreck who filled his pockets with his own gold drowned as consequence of their weight. It is our relationships with what we buy that matters. The valuable is possessed by the valiant. In the illustration to the left the necklace is an expression of love and valuable for that reason, and without valour the valuable is not realized in practice. Without the affectionate element in human nature we are nothing. We are not motivated chiefly by pay or financial inducement, but by spirit. Affection becomes credible when it is seemingly selfless and directed towards others. This falsifies all of the economists' results. Ruskin annoyed many contemporaries. One anonymous reviewer complained that reading his work was like "being preached to death by a mad governess." But he had a major influence on Leo Tolstoy, William Morris, Mahatma Gandhi and others. His style is conveyed by the quotation below.

"Observe I neither impugn nor doubt the conclusions of the science (of economics) I am simply uninterested in them, as I would be of a science of gymnastics which claimed that men had no skeletons. It might be shown on that supposition that it would be advantageous to roll students up into pellets, flatten them into cakes and stretch them into cables, and that when these results were effected, the re-insertion of the skeleton would be attended by certain inconveniences to the constitution. The reasoning might be admirable, the conclusions true and the science defective only in its applicability."

HOW IS CAPITALISM EVOLVING?
TWO PROBLEMS AT LEAST

THE UNIT OF SURVIVAL IS THE PERSON
PLUS THE ENVIRONMENT

CONSUMPTION IS DEVOURING THE PRODUCTIVE ETHOS

There are two major barriers to the evolution of capitalism depicted opposite. In the first place the unit of survival and evolution is NOT the person on his/her own. The individual only survives with the support of an environment. Even assuming life is a battlefield, the field must be nurtured, not assailed, otherwise it will cease to support life. The second issue is that post-capitalism is increasingly consumer-oriented. We have to indulge more and more, devour more and more just to keep the economy going! Immigrants flock to the countries where these levels of consumption are the highest. Obesity now rivals malnutrition as a killer. We work so as to stop working! The orientation to consumption is the antithesis of the orientation to production; no wonder we have a productivity crisis. No wonder the UK and Australia score highest in self-indulgence in the world and China scores highest in self-discipline. We extol ingestion and becoming alimentary canals. We have to eat to live, but should we live to eat, distributing cheap money and indebtedness? Progress is not a straight line but a learning loop, Oedipus tapping the ground before him with a stick to augment his lack of vision.

THE PHENOMENON OF "CHIMERICA"

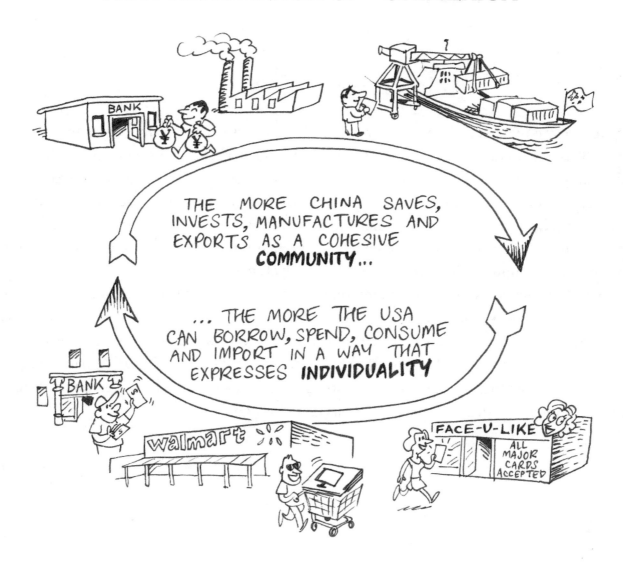

A DIVISION OF LABOUR LETHAL TO THE WEST.

Another problem with straight-line thinking is that we do not see the circle and what it is doing to us. The global division of labour between the USA and China can do the former a lot of harm. According to Niall Ferguson and Moritz Schularick, China increasingly specializes in saving, investment, manufacturing and exporting as a cohesive community, while America increasingly specializes borrowing, spending, consuming and importing in ways that express the individuality of its people. The two processes are symbiotic. Americans borrow what the Chinese save, they spend on what China has invested in, consume what the Chinese produce, and import what the Chinese export, leading the latter to a huge balance of payments surplus so that they hold vast amounts of US treasury bills. It used not to be possible to consume excessively without spurring inflation. Interest rates would need to be hiked to choke-off spending, but the cheap exports from China meant the West could spend without this inflation occurring, as they were so cheap. It is much easier to individualize yourself by shopping in a personalized style than by working, which is typically done in groups. Yet this specialization erodes national character. To define yourself by what you consume is to choose passivity, appetite and self-indulgence. To define yourself by what you produce is to choose pro-action, restraint and self- discipline. A person whose insatiability lands him/her deeply in debt is a hostage to economic events, greatly limited in life-choices. If we wanted China to leave us in its wake we could hardly do more to bring this about.

e) THE FALLACY OF THE MORE THE BETTER: THINKING IN STRAIGHT LINES

REASON IS A POOR GUIDE IF YOUR PREMISES ARE FALSE.

One problem with believing that money and profit are an unalloyed good is that it reduces values to imaginary things and conceives of progress as linear. We seize on a single principle and try to maximize it. Getting ever richer, getting ever stronger and more secure, getting ever more powerful, ever more intelligent, moving faster than anyone else. All such aims merely incite others to match you and if possible to bring you down. But more importantly, the Single Principle grows so grandiose that it ignores its value contrast. The ability to condemn the world's people to a nuclear winter through hydrogen weapons makes all of us weaker and more impotent, grabbing what we can on borrowed time. We cannot be supremely tough as Trump tries to be, without forgoing tenderness and vulnerability. We cannot be rich without taking away the money needed far more urgently by others. We can't be powerful without disempowering others. We cannot be victorious without leaving losers in the dust behind us. We cannot prove that we are supremely intelligent without shrinking the concept to a singular dimension that ignores diversity and obscures other talents. This rule applies to soft values as well as hard. If you love your persecutors that can enrage them, make them feel morally inferior. If you forgive them they may feel this is an insult. If you put flowers in gun barrels the soldiers will want you dead! Nothing, not even love, should be pursued unilaterally. It will end in tragedy. "Nothing to Excess" was written on the base of the statue of Athena in the Parthenon and we ignore it at our peril. Many examples follow.

THE DREAM OF UNBRIDLED POWER AND STRENGTH

AS THE POWER TO DESTROY GROWS, IT ENVELOPS ITS PERPETRATORS.

The clearest example of the suicidal nature of linear thinking is the notion that our strength can be increased without limit to make us impregnable. It is the temptation of the serpent in the Garden of Eden, save that the godlike power is that of destruction, not creation. The USA now has more weaponry than the next five nations in the world, but far from this making it stronger, it leads to counter-threats from Islamic extremists, otherwise insignificant opponents. The prospect of death did not deter the destruction of the Twin Towers. That America could destroy the world hundreds of times over does not make it any stronger than killing us all just once. Nor is it possible to destroy the earth as a habitat and not destroy ourselves. Our children's children, if we get that far, will look back at us in amazement. We stockpiled weapons and our fondest hope was that they would be utterly useless, even while a third of the world was malnourished. There is only one path to greater strength, that of making ourselves psychologically vulnerable to the views of others. All values split from their contrasts are pathological. Killing others will not spare us the deaths of all. Hephaestus, blacksmith to the gods, was the only flawed immortal. He limped. Technology unbalances us and makes some of our endowments disproportionately huge.

SHOULD WE ALL STRIVE TO BE WINNERS?

WINNERS PRE-SUPPOSE LOSERS.

Should we all strive to be winners? Is winning and not losing what life is all about? It is glaringly obvious that winning involves other people being forced to lose. Indeed, the losers typically out-number the winners, so are we choosing a society in which most persons lose? When we distinguish ourselves are we casting others into the shadows? For every hopeful film star how many people have been told, "Don't call us, we'll call you!"? And the phone never rang. What saves us from utterly crushing each other's spirits is diversity, what it is we win at. There is no reason why a chess champion, a star engineer and a golf pro should not appreciate each other's abilities with no trace of envy. Each is good at what they value. And in no way does the success of one detract from the success of others, so different are their abilities. But the important point at issue is that values come in pairs and one will always trigger the other. You cannot just have winners, successes, joyfulness and hope. They come with losers, failures, woe and disappointment and inflicting this on others is of doubtful benefit. The intensity of these experiences grows out of the contrasts between them; winning after losing and succeeding after failing are the more vivid and memorable. One thing about commercial and personal relationships is the possibility that sellers and buyers or each partner both win or wins. Where the sun is directly overhead there is no shadow. Much of this book is about win-win relationships of people so different that engaging them is a pleasing experience of novelty and we do not begrudge their unique excellence at all. A man who has his legs amputated below the knee and wins a wheelchair race is excellent in his own way.

❧

Winning by carving off pieces of China

"A war more unjust in its origins, a war more calculated in its progress to cover this country in permanent disgrace, cannot be imagined."

William Gladstone

A century of humiliation.

The idea that certain nations can make the rules that others must obey was never more clearly exemplified than in the Opium Wars, 1837-42 and 1856-60, ostensibly excused as support for free trade. China, as today, had a large balance of trade surplus with the West. The latter wanted its fine porcelain, silk and other aesthetic products. The Chinese did not want our cheap cotton goods. So Britain shipped opium grown in its Indian colonies to China, where it addicted an estimated 30 million Chinese and made Britain an international drugs-runner. The war broke out when the opium was seized. Wooden Chinese war-junks were shot out the water by steel ships of the East India Company. In the subsequent Nanking Treaty, Hong Kong was ceded to the British in perpetuity. William Gladstone put it well, "A war more unjust in its origins, a war more calculated in its progress to cover this country in permanent disgrace, cannot be imagined." For the Chinese, this began the "Century of Humiliation", which is illustrated opposite with European powers carving up the Chinese dragon between them. We would not try to impose such rules today, would we? We quote from Trump's most recent demands to the Chinese, as summarized by Martin Wolf in the *Financial Times.* "China is to take concrete and viable steps to reduce the China-US trade imbalance by $100 billion in the 12 months beginning in June 2018 and by another $100 billion by June 2019...China is not to avail itself of due process or ask for justice...China will withdraw its request for WTO consultations relating to tariff actions on intellectual property...and will not take any retaliatory action in response to actions taken or to be taken by the US, including any new US restriction...China will not oppose, challenge or retaliate against US imposition of restrictions... China will withdraw its complaints to the WTO." For such demands to be met, the Chinese government would need to end its market system. We are trying to inflict humiliation once more.

THE LINEAR HARPOON AND THE GREAT WHITE WHALE

WE ARE INEXTRICABLY TIED TO OUR ENVIRONMENT

It is the extraordinary distinction of American classical literature that it warns of the excesses of the writer's own culture from *The Scarlet Letter,* to *The Masque of the Red Death,* to *The Great Gatsby.* Opposite we look at the climatic ending of *Moby Dick* by Herman Melville who died in disappointment and was posthumously heralded for this and other symbolic novels. Captain Ahab commands a whaling ship. When a whale is spotted it is typically surrounded by long boats and harpoons are thrown into its thrashing body until it eventually expires and its blubber harvested. Ahab is a man possessed by an encounter with an abnormally large, white whale named Moby Dick. An earlier attempt to kill it cost him a leg and like so many villains he limps on a wooden stump. When this whale is sighted he loses all sense of proportion or commercial common sense, or mercy for another captain's son swept overboard. He will hunt down and will personally spear his mortal foe. Moby Dick for its part is quite indifferent to Ahab, until the first harpoons strikes him, whereupon he goes berserk with fury. It is man's straight-line purpose with its cruel barbs against God's creation. We attack our environment and it will turn on us. Ahab hurls his harpoon and it pierces the whale. However, the fast unravelling coil of rope inside the boat catches his ankle and he finds himself strapped to side of the creature by his own harpoon rope. We are joined to God's creation whether we wish it or no. The whale now turns on the ship itself, rams and sinks it. Only one man escapes to tell the tale, saved by clinging to a wooden coffin. We are warned that our way of thinking is dangerously obsessive. Getting our singular way is full of peril. That the eye of the whale is the world itself we have borrowed from the genius of Gerald Scarfe, the English cartoonist.

❦

ABSOLUTE VALUES ARE PALPABLY ABSURD - WE SHOULD LAUGH

"ALL IDOLS SOONER OR LATER BECOME MOLOCHS, HUNGRY FOR HUMAN SACRIFICE" ALDOUS HUXLEY

We should laugh at absolute values. They lead to exactly the opposite of what they intend. If we do not laugh we may soon cry. Saki (H.H. Monroe) has a bachelor in a railway compartment telling a story to two little girls, after their aunt appears to have bored them with her stories of very good girls. He starts off with one of the aunt's specimens. "There was once a little girl called Bertha who was so good that she was awarded three medals, one for Obedience, one for Punctuality and one for Good Conduct." The two little girls, initially hopeful, slump back into weary resignation. "In fact, Bertha was horribly good." The little girls perk up at this phrase. "The Prince of that country hearing of Bertha's goodness invited her to walk in his garden overrun as it was with little pigs. Bertha was congratulating herself as she walked through the garden when a great grey wolf loped into the garden, hoping to eat a pig but preferring Bertha. Greatly alarmed she hid in a myrtle bush which smelled so strong the wolf could not detect her. She would have escaped had not the medal for Obedience clinked against the medal for Punctuality which clinked against the medal for Good Conduct. As it was, the wolf was able to find her and eat her up." The aunt is aghast at this story. But the eldest of the little girls opined, "the story started badly but had a wonderful ending." Is the moral of this story that little girls are really monsters underneath, happy to see one of them devoured? We prefer to think that it is the ideal of the ever punctual, obedient little girl that is so stupid, so impossible and so oppressive that it deserves to devoured forthwith. No child could live up to it and would be an impossible little prig if she tried, as indeed was Bertha. Children often err (thank God) and learn from such experience. The ideals held up to them lead to exactly the opposite from that which adults intended. Is this the "unconscious" or the folly of an absolute value beneath which the contrasting value lies? Do we routinely extol "horribly good" conduct?

THINKING IN STRAIGHT LINES 1: ABSTRACT GLOBALISM

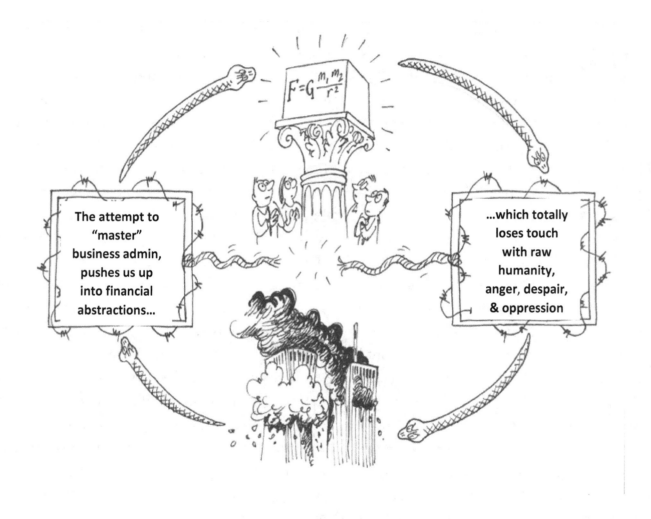

The attempt to "master" business admin, pushes us up into financial abstractions...

...which totally loses touch with raw humanity, anger, despair, & oppression

NOT EVERYBODY WANTS TO OBEY AMERICA'S RULES.

When you think about it, the ambition to "master" business administration is very strange. Is there really a body of coherent knowledge that teaches us how best to run both a funeral parlour and produce high frequency transducers? Could this possibly be taught in two years by reading and discussing written cases? Almost inevitably these claims to mastery end up favouring global finance and accountancy which is one thing all international businesses must have, preferably in common. It is but a small step from here to want finance to rule the world. Education in Germany, France, Scandinavia and much of Asia, teaches industrial practice first and then management within these vocations. There are scant claims to universality. What MBA education is really about is an attempt to make those handling the money made by America's great entrepreneurs look respectable. What right has a side-kick of Andrew Carnegie to dispose of his wealth? What qualifies him/her to do this? MBA courses were needed to answer such questions and because the money was already there, they taught how to handle these resources, not the genius that created the wealth it in the first place. Today MBAs tend to go into finance rather than industry and few industries can afford them. That creative industries like Silicon Valley avoids MBAs tells its own story. High-tech entrepreneurs suffer from a variation of the same problem, their pet algorithm must conquer the world like Uber's system of summoning taxis. What is not admitted is that much of its success comes from turning driving into casual labour and moving money from workers to owners. When the magic formula reaps a whirlwind, we simply cling more tenaciously to the latest formula and call those who object Luddites. It is a form of idolatry. The Twin Towers were the most visible manifestation of American universalism. They begot a suicidal, nihilistic, very cruel rage among those left outside the system. Have we bought the Age of Trump upon ourselves?

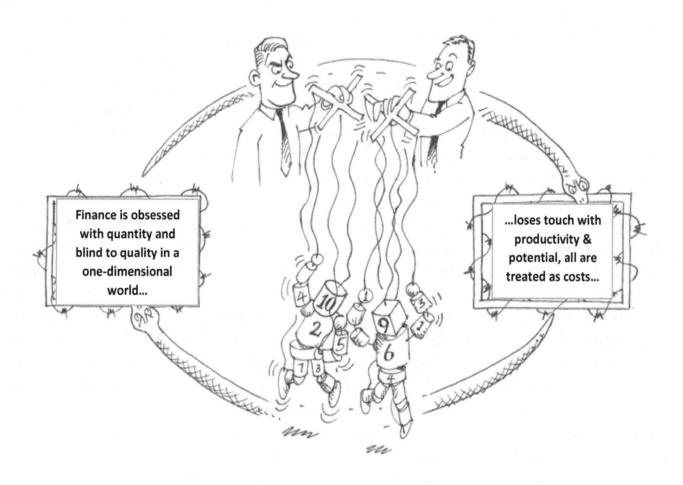

Finance is obsessed with quantity and blind to quality in a one-dimensional world...

...loses touch with productivity & potential, all are treated as costs...

THAT DOES NOT COUNT.

One of the besetting problems of American and British industry is the myth of managing by numbers and the rise of the bean-counters. These people think in straight lines, lower wages, less cost, less tax equals more profit. This puts all the emphasis on quantity and neglects quality. This is despite that fact that all quantity is OF a particular quality. For example, a Ford Pinto gas tank that does not burst into flames in a rear-end collision has a very different quality from one that does. Yet the decision not to modify the tank was taken on the basis that this would cost $137 million while litigation costs associated with being sued would only be about $45.9 million. The qualities of the two tanks were assumed to be the same! Not having your children incinerated in the back seat was seen as irrelevant. The scandal was exposed by Ralph Nader in his book, *Unsafe at any Speed* and Ford was investigated by the Senate and forced to issue a public apology. Robert McNamara who had been in charge of Ford's managing-by-numbers campaign took its lessons to the Vietnam War where he instituted the notorious body-count. If we killed more of them we would win, right? No one asked how many Vietnamese might change sides where so many civilians were killed. We were swelling enemy numbers with our "free fire zones"! No one asked if they had a purpose and a passion which our side lacked, whether national pride has a place in human affairs.

At the roots of the numbers game is that what you are measuring are more like objects than people, more like numbered puppets than flesh and blood. You can count them from afar and from above. When Carly Fiorina became CEO of Hewlett-Packard, one of the most admired companies in the USA, she slashed R&D, declared 15,000 people redundant, cut worker salaries and all meaningful innovation ceased. She awarded herself a $65 million stock package. When she was forced out a few years later the stock price had halved. John Sculley was a numbers man from Pepsi. Steve Jobs hired him to run Apple and he was fired for his pains for not adhering to those numbers. Clearly the man's quality was not a consideration. Note that the fallacy illustrated is self-perpetuating. As business stagnates, the obsession with cutting costs grows. The need to be "in control" mounts. Employees must obey, hence the vicious circle.

ARE WE FIGHTING PEOPLE OR SERVING THEM?

IS STRATEGY MILITANT, MUTUAL,
OR BOTH

Strategy thinking has difficulty deciding whether it is preponderantly competitive or cooperative. The truth is that both must be present. You compete with your rivals at cooperating with your customers. Until you start serving customers there is nothing to compete about! If serving customers is a mere means to the end of competing fiercely then it is unlikely to be done very well. Your first impulse must be to be of service to others and competing grows out of this. In cultures where the competitive ethic is very strong, customers get deceived, assailed and manipulated, see right of illustration. Competing becomes mis-directed and promiscuous. We will outwit everyone! It is generally easier to fool the consumer than a bunch of fellow professionals as well organized as oneself. The result is that many banks cooperate with each other to strategically outwit customers. Given asymmetries of knowledge and information it is much easier to fool the naïve than a fellow predator. Banks make it impossible to compare charges because they do not wish their customers to know this and complex cash-back rewards schemes and hidden charges make their offerings incomparable, together with the hassle of switching. It would probably pay them to give free computer lessons in online banking but imagination is often the first casualty in competitive strategic thinking. Note that empowering women might be aspects of any remedy. They do most shopping and buying. If they demanded certain information on fairness, they would get it! The internet gives customers opportunities to organize and publish information on the social character of supplying organisations.

TOP-DOWN ORDERS LEAD TO MUD, BLOOD AND FUTILITY

THE NOTION OF BRILLIANT STRATEGY

Henry Mintzberg has compared much top-down, cleverly designed corporate strategy to the Battle of Passchendaele in World War I in which there were 60,000 casualties in the first twenty minutes. Final casualties on both sides are estimated at three quarters of a million. The General Staff, miles behind the front line, had no idea that that battlefield was completely water-logged. It had been raining non-stop for two weeks. A large number of advancing troops actually drowned in water-filled craters. As a cavalry officer, Field Marshall Sir Douglas Haig wanted to punch a hole in enemy lines large enough to send in the horses! Strategy designed on high runs into the following difficulties. It is too rigid and predictable. If the enemy uses identical strategy it ends in a bloody stalemate. It cannot learn or digest bad news and change its mind. It is ludicrously abstract and cerebral. It takes too long to execute and is clearly visible. It stops those on the ground from thinking for themselves. It never pauses to reconsider the premises on which it is based. It answers every doubt by prescribing more of the same. It subscribes to racist dogma that our soldiers are braver and brighter than theirs and must prevail in the end. When a junior staff officer eventually visited the battlefield he burst into tears, "to think we sent them into battle in that!" Designed strategy loses all touch with the actual environment which is there to be blasted into submission and blown sky-high. Finally, it is steeled against all compassion. "My subject is war and the pity of war," wrote Wilfred Owen. "The poetry is in the pity." It is the poetry which has survived.

WHY LINEAR STRATEGIES FAIL: NO WORLD-BEATING STRATEGY IS POSSIBLE

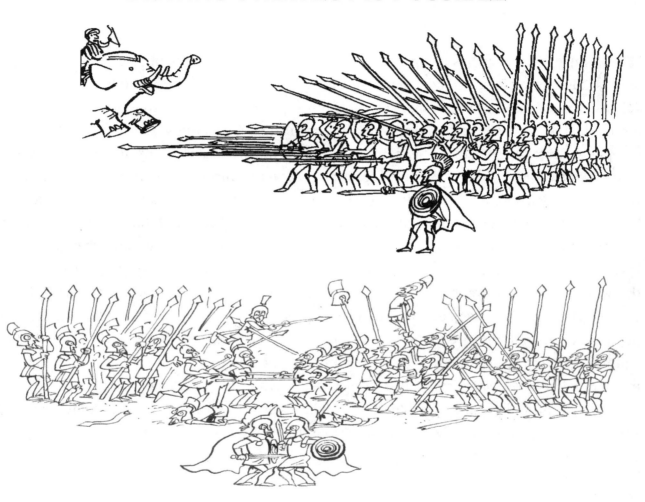

IDENTICAL STRATEGIES LEAD TO BLOODY WARS OF ATTRITION.

Alexander the Great conquered the known world by dint of a strategy of spears and shields called a phalanx, with the strategos as the officer in charge. It beat every army it encountered, even Indian elephants. Yet when he died his generals could not agree on how to share the empire and phalanx turned on phalanx with the result seen in the lower picture, the shortest empire ever! The moral is that strategies succeed by being novel and unknown by your opponent, so no sooner is a strategy imitated than the rot sets in as armies clash in battles of mutual attrition. This helps explain the boom and bust in electronics early this century. Many companies copied Amazon in buying market share quickly while sustaining heavy losses to attract customers and try to dominate a particular market. But when many companies do this at the same time they cut each other's throats and the whole industry suffers. Amazon succeeded because it was original and successfully competed with bookshops, not because buying market share is a brilliant move under all circumstances! We will see later that a strategy must be novel to be successful. No sooner do opponents discover what your strategy is, then it is easily countered. In Alexander's day, news did not travel.

STRAIGHT-LINE STRATEGIES LEAD US STRAIGHT INTO CONTRADICTION

EVERY STRAIGHT-LINE STRATEGY HAS ITS DIRECT NEGATION ACCORDING TO BOB DE WITT AND RON MEYER. WE HEAD STRAIGHT FOR AN IMPASSE

TEN CONTRADICTIONS

1. Strategy is *rational* thought (Kenneth Andrews)

1. Strategy is *generative* (Kenichi Ohmae)

2. Strategy is *pre- planned* (Balaji Chakravarthy)

2. Strategy is *emergent* (Henry Mintzberg & James Quinn)

3. Strategic re-*engineering* should obliterate the old (Michael Hammer)

3. Strategy should *refine* and *preserve* what is old (Masaaki Imai)

4. Strategy is *market-driven* (Michael Porter)

4. Strategy is *capability-driven* (George Stalk, Philip Evans)

5. Strategic business units constitute a *portfolio* (Barry Hedley)

5. Strategic business units constitute a *core competence* (CK Prahalad, Gary Hamel)

6. Strategy is primarily *competitive* among discrete BUs (Gary Hamel, Yves Doz, CK Prahalad)

6. Strategy is primarily *cooperative* among networked BUs (Gianni Lorenzoni, Charles Baden-Fuller)

7. Strategy is *evolutionary* via natural selection (Michael Porter)

7. Strategy is *creative* with new rules of the game (C. Baden-Fuller & John Stopford)

8. Strategy is the triumph of *control* over the company (R. Christensen, J Bower)

8. Strategy encounters *chaos* from which new order emerges (Ralph Stacey)

9. Strategy posits global *convergence* (Theodore Levitt)

9. Strategy posits *diversity* and localization of markets (Susan Douglas, Yorand Wind)

10. Strategy must be tied to profitability of *shareholders* (Alfred Rappaport)

10. Strategy should optimize *stakeholder* interests and gains (Edward R Freeman & David Reed)

To avoid these head-on collisions, turn to the next page.

ALL VIABLE BUSINESS STRATEGIES ARE CIRCULAR, NOT STRAIGHT LINES

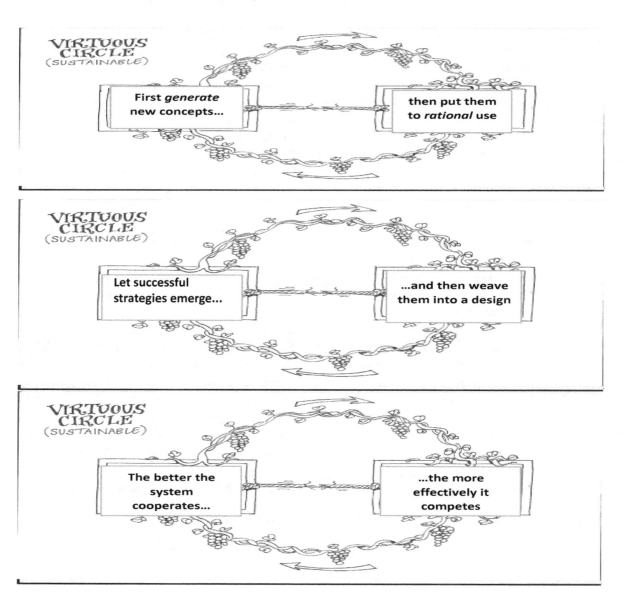

Unless business strategies are circular, there is no feedback from the front line of operations and they cannot learn whether they are effective or ineffective. In our first virtuous circle opposite we must first generate a new concept, say heavier-than-air flight, and then develop rational and logical means to carry this through. The logic used to generate the initial breakthrough is different from the logic used to implement the discovery and help buyers to use it. The proof that heavier-than-air flight is possible is a logic re-constructed after the fact. Rationality is a process used to test and prove a proposition, not to invent it initially. It is the same with letting strategies emerge from what customers say they want and what they are satisfied with when this is supplied, see second picture opposite. We now have a set of practices known to work. We know our employees can do this and we know customers are content with this, so that is the moment to weave them into a more elegant strategic design whose parts are known to work and to join these parts to form a seamless whole. If a team first cooperates in passing the ball swiftly between team members, see third picture opposite, then it will better compete with rival teams or rival companies.

This works for all the seeming contradictions on the previous page. You start with a portfolio of products you make or have acquired. Then you look for a common theme or core competence among these, and build up a set of mutually supporting products and services, selling off the remainder. You first develop your capability and take it to the market, let chaos wash over you and bring controlled order to this, build better relations with all stakeholders and pay the residue to shareholders, be creative but realize that the environment may force your products to evolve and trigger accidental developments. You first exemplify diversity by generating a surplus of propositions and then converge on the best possible solutions among these. Note that which of these contrasting values are put first, is a crucial issue. You can create first and then use reason, but if you only stick to reason you will not create. You can organize your portfolio into a core competence, but do not disorganise your core competence into a portfolio, unless you seek to fail. Some sequences ARE reversible. For example, you can compete to come up with the best idea and then cooperate to turn it into action.

The Rise of the Unicorn

Original sketch by Penelope Hampden-Turner

Private, innovative, unicorn companies have no truck with shareholders

What is a Unicorn Company? It has been precisely defined by Aileen Lee as an innovative, private tech company with an assessed value of $1 billion (£750,000) or more. There are 227 active Unicorns in the world today, with 57 added in 2018, so that these are growing by as much as 25% annually. The largest Unicorns like Uber (worth $69 billion), Airbnb ($31 billion) and WeWork ($40 billion) are very much in the news. Alibaba was a Unicorn before it went public. China has the most Unicorns of any country and also the lowest proportion going public, as befits its family ethos. The UK has 13 Unicorns worth over £18 billion and leads Europe in this respect.

Why are they called Unicorns? They were originally scarce and near mythical in their unexpected appearance and mysterious characters. Several have grown at amazing speed and have huge estimates of value while never once making a profit! Their whole future is a matter of estimate and conjecture, and is somehow unreal, Uber and Airbnb being among these. They are important to the theme of this book in that they show that innovative companies avoid going public and letting shareholders into their business models. Shareholders want profits, while many Unicorns register losses as they go for cut prices to gain high market share, and put all their revenues into research and rapid growth. (Amazon made losses for several years on end). This clearly indicates several facts. Most shareholders cannot be trusted to grow a company. They want to extract its money. An increasing number of high-tech firms issue non-voting shares or give the shares held by the founding family ten times the votes. They are determined not be slowed down by profit-taking. They want to see the most innovative persons in charge of the company. In addition, there is no shortage of capital for such companies. Those estimating its value in many billions are more than happy to subscribe. An Initial Public Offering would make the founders rich but many prefer a life of creativity and innovation to piles of money. Their early losses are a long-term investment in a future of invention-without-end.

PART II

WEALTH CREATION
AND
WEALTH DESTRUCTION

a) HOW THE WEALTH-CREATING CYCLE WORKS

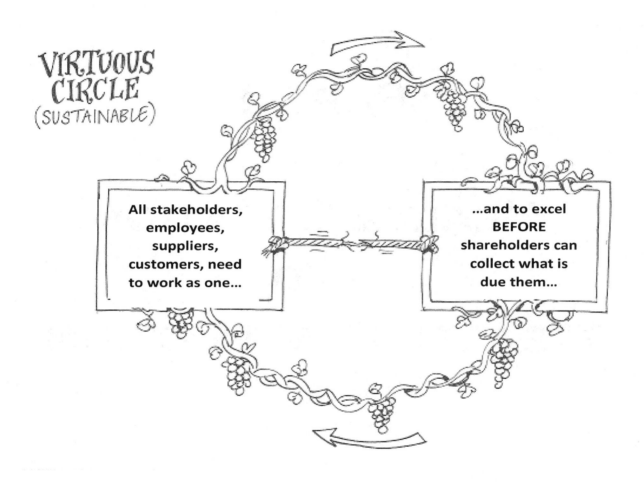

VIRTUOUS CIRCLE (SUSTAINABLE)

All stakeholders, employees, suppliers, customers, need to work as one...

...and to excel BEFORE shareholders can collect what is due them...

SHAREHOLDERS GET MORE BY WAITING.

It is surely as plain as the nose on your face that various stakeholders, employees, suppliers, customers, the community, government and the environment must first generate wealth BEFORE those who hold equity shares are to reap any benefit from this activity. Shareholders can only receive the revenue customers have contributed, assuming the latter are well satisfied with what employees and suppliers have produced. To what degree might stakeholders excel? We do not really know this until we have chosen the best employees, paid them well, invited them to be innovative, spent heavily on R&D to give them better tools, equipment and sponsored new discoveries. All this will depend on suppliers getting us the best available raw materials and components and helping us to make the most of these. If we do not help and nurture suppliers, they cannot excel. We also need to be close to customers and, if possible, co-create with them so that they help us do even better. Promising money for shareholders before we have seen what stakeholders might achieve if properly equipped and encouraged, is a serious error. We will now go through the segments one by one.

THE CIRCULAR PROCESS OF WEALTH CREATION

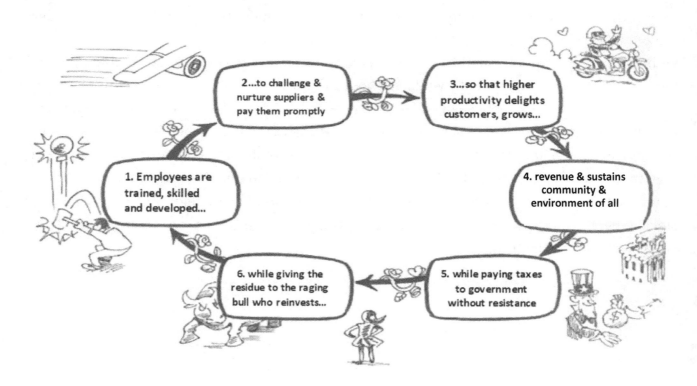

1. Employees are trained, skilled and developed...

2...to challenge & nurture suppliers & pay them promptly

3...so that higher productivity delights customers, grows...

4. revenue & sustains community & environment of all

5. while paying taxes to government without resistance

6. while giving the residue to the raging bull who reinvests...

This illustration is the virtuous circle of wealth creation. We apologise for its obviousness. It is in reality a helix since: 1. Employees may develop and learn more and more. 2. Suppliers can constantly improve in the quality of what they supply. 3. Customers are increasingly delighted and empowered so that revenue climbs and 4. stakeholders and the shared environment are sustained. 5. Taxes are paid without expensive resistance. Finally owing to the quality of segments 1-5 there is 6, a handsome residue for shareholders which pays our pensions. Despite earlier reservations, we are not against shareholders receiving their due. What we are against is shareholders pushing to the front of the line and receiving a priority over those who must create the wealth BEFORE there is any for shareholders to collect. It is not until employees and suppliers have produced, grateful customers have upped their purchases, and government has been paid for its supportive role, that there is any money for shareholders to receive. Moreover, the amount collected will crucially depend on how well other stakeholders have been treated and how innovative and productive they have become in their work. If their resources have been depleted, their efforts may wilt.

Where does wealth come from? It comes from assembling components so that the "house" is worth more than a pile of bricks, wood and plaster. It comes from the pleasure of inhabiting the house and having a home which is more than an empty building. It is segments 1-4 in the cycle above which creates more than the parties began with and which shareholders, were they wise, would support. What the government gets and shareholders get will subtract from what others receive, but what those in the other four segments get between them grows the pie. To treat employees, suppliers and customers well is to unleash their potential and reap the benefits. We will now go through these segments one by one to see what successful companies have accomplished.

1. EMPLOYEES ARE TRAINED, SKILLED, EDUCATED, DEVELOPED AND KEPT WELL

MUCH CHEAPER TO MAINTAIN THE EMPLOYEE'S HEALTH THEN WAIT FOR THEM TO FALL ILL.

Opposite, we depict employees who are not the units of labour beloved by some economists. They grow, they learn, they discover, create, innovate and excel, depending on the care and attention they receive from those who manage them and the size of the budgets for R&D and training. What they thrive on is respect and encouragement and appeals to what is inside them, rather than cash bonuses. For example, United Parcel Services, (UPS), is the largest and one of the most profitable delivery companies in the world. In 1999 alone, it helped 20,000 part-time employees with their college educations. All employees are eligible for $25,000 college bursaries. They get free health insurance, even if working part time. A waste of shareholders' money? What is the effect of having ambitious young people seek you out? When they get the jobs their educations qualified them for, whose service will they choose for the rest of their lives? UPS shareholders have nothing to complain of!

Johnson and Johnson's credo dating from 1943 states, "shareholders come last" and yet over the years few companies have been more generous to their shareholders and to all those with a stake in their success. Johnson and Johnson has a famous Wellness Program for employees, entirely voluntary yet massively subscribed to. It is vastly cheaper to keep employees well through monitoring than to wait for them to fall sick and pay the bills. It reckons that every dollar spent on wellness, saves two dollars on health insurance, absenteeism, sickness. The time to stop drinking is before you wreck your life and your career. The time to stop over-eating is before you get morbidly obese, lose your friends and eat more to comfort yourself. Jordan's Furniture is among many who pay employees 20% or more above the industry average, yet their productivity and sales per person are 40% higher and their training hours double. Everyone is better off. Google provides on-site physicians, free massages, a game room, free gourmet lunches, counselling on tax and legal services. Toyota in Kentucky offers 24-hour child care to manual workers, has a free gym, a Wellness centre and employee activity centre of 19,000 square feet. Patagonia pays up to $2,000 of the cost of green vehicles purchased by its employees. Wegmans employs single mothers as baggers and offers to train them for jobs in management. Every year Fortune magazine publishes the "100 best companies to work for". These are nominated by employees. These 100 companies are three times more profitable than the S&P 500 average.

2. SUPPLIERS ARE CHALLENGED, NURTURED, DEVELOPED AND MADE PROSPEROUS

DON'T SELL THE JET ENGINE, SELL ITS PERFORMANCE

In order to appreciate just how much a supplier can do for a customer, we have to look at Business2Business relationships, since these are deeper and have often greater integrity than does consumer marketing. Suppose you are selling a jet engine to an airline, the engine itself standing in the warehouse has little value for the airline. What is valuable is the use to which the engine is put conveying paying passengers from one airport to another. If it works but needs more maintenance and repair than foreseen, then the customer may be out of money. If it does not last as it is supposed to and has to be replaced, then the airline also suffers. If the engine is delivered and then wrongly installed the customer is also disappointed. How then can we have the best possible relationship between supplier and customer, one in which both parties can have full confidence and one that is guaranteed to deliver the value promised? Full value is received if the supplier sells not the engine but the result of using the engine properly, the power by the hour which the engine delivers. Since the supplier made the engine, he knows all about its installation, inspection, maintenance and repair, and the relationship is much more satisfactory if he takes responsibility for seeing that this is done and money he receives is conditional on everything working as it was supposed to. Treating suppliers well so they treat customers well is sheer common sense, they provide 50% and up of the product or the service you are selling. The more competent they are, the more useful your final offering to your customer, in this case the airline passenger. Michael Porter reports that Nestlé has increased the income of coffee and coco farmers by 200-300% by helping them select, dry, store and maintain the quality of their beans. Nestlé benefits too. If you develop your suppliers you will get the full benefit of their added expertise. In the automobile industry, most innovation is in electronics supplied from the outside. Your suppliers are the pioneers.

3. HIGHER PRODUCTIVITY THAT DELIGHTS CUSTOMERS & INCREASES REVENUE

THESE COMPANIES WERE ALL LOVED BY THEIR CUSTOMERS

Harley Davidson is an iconic brand with fanatically loyal fans. It is unionized but treats the union as a partner. The company nearly succumbed in the 80s and 13 managers bought it out from AFM and turned it around. It has refused for many years to lay off a single employee. But its major success is with customers who are dedicated missionaries for the brand. The Harley Owners' Club acted as an intermediary between dealers and the company. It scarcely ever advertises and relies on word of mouth and personal relationships among fans. The Harley Davidson Learning Centre believes in continuous improvement with many ideas for improvement coming from customers. Employees are given enough autonomy and discretion to make absolutely certain the customer is satisfied. The company is close to being a life-style. If we want to understand wealth creation, then customer-relations are a clue. A motor-cycle can become a delivery service and pay for itself fifty times over.

A group of researchers at Bentley College, headed by Raj Sisodia, asked a most unusual research question. They asked respondents to nominate a company they truly loved - not liked, admired or respected but loved. They got hundreds of nominations but whittled these down to thirty or so with wide recognition. Some of the companies nominated are featured opposite. Others not illustrated include Whole Foods, Costco, Wegmans, Toyota, Southwest Airlines, UPS, 3M, Jordan's Furniture, IDEO, LL Bean, REI, Timberland and The Motley Fool. These are part of the Conscious Capitalism movement and all believe that care bestowed on stakeholders will result in better returns for shareholders, that capitalism needs to be conscious of all the benefits it confers and turn this into overt strategy. A similar movement is the rise of Benefit Corporations, of which there are now more than one thousand in the US alone. These change their bye-laws to make benefit to the society a prime objective and profiting a means to this. Over 30 US states have passed legislation welcoming B Corporations, in by-partisan initiatives. Liberals love B Corporations because of the values they symbolize, but Conservatives love them too. They always said private enterprise could do it!

4. THIS GROWS LOCAL COMMUNITIES & SUSTAINS THE ENVIRONMENT...

LIFTING NATURE TO THE ROOFTOPS.

If you run a business in an amazing world full of powerful natural forces like wind, sun and tide then surely harnessing your needs and wants to these natural forces makes abundant sense? But it takes a whole community of stakeholders to make companies sustainable. We need employees to eliminate waste, save energy and work smarter. We need suppliers to know exactly what is in the raw material they supply and rid this of toxins. We need customers to sort the waste from what they consume and help to recycle it. The image opposite envisages cities turned green. All flat roofs are potential platforms for flower or vegetable gardens, for solar or wind energy, and for recreation. A building with a garden on its roof is cooler in summer and warmer in winter, according to McDonough and Braungart. Its fruits can be shared by occupants and visitors. IKEA has turned its warehouse-size shopping centres into solar energy generators and sells surpluses back to the grid. There is no inherent reason why our cities should not turn green and resemble the Hanging Gardens of Babylon, one of the Seven Wonders of the Ancient World. What we are seeking is nothing less than the harmonization of nature and the built environment.

We must distinguish between re-cycling, down-cycling and up-cycling. The last two get their names from whether the residue and waste from the product is less valuable or more valuable than the product itself. The scrap from old cars can go to support concrete (down-cycling), but if stripped of impurities it can go back into new cars (recycling). Animal slurry can be turned into nitrate fertilizer (up-cycling). When a product is initially designed, a second life and use of what is left over can be purposefully engineered. This is branch of innovation is called up-cycling and fuses with nature.

5. ...WHILE PAYING TAXES TO GOVERNMENT WITHOUT RESISTANCE

REPAYING THE GOVERNMENT FOR ITS SPONSORSHIP OF PUBLIC GOODS

The money we pay in taxes to government should be a voluntary contribution on behalf of the nation and all tax-payers, and an appreciation of grants to education, to the armed forces, to the basic research needed by science, infrastructure, to federal courts, to policing, to welfare, to the space programme, to public health, to foreign aid and to world diplomatic leadership in general. Much of it was recently given to the banking sector to bail out the wealthy who had gambled it away. Unlike charity, government money is received without a great burden of moral indebtedness upon the recipient. The 28 stakeholder-sustaining, highly profitable companies selected by Mackey and Sisodia and Sisodia, Wolfe and Seth in *Firms of Endearment* all paid corporate taxes without mounting legal resistance. They acknowledged what they owed to their nation and to fellow citizens. The vitriolic denunciation of government was nowhere in evidence. The US faces unusually high corporate tax-burden, currently being cut by Donald Trump, but this is met by massive legal avoidance, with lawyers who outnumber and may have more resources than those the government can marshal. The net result is that only a fraction of the official tax rate is actually paid and the idea that private enterprise fights government for its survival is perpetuated. The US government has historically done much to boost the economy. The years of fastest economic growth were spurred by expenditure in two world wars, the Cold War, the Korean War and Vietnam War, which also boosted Japan, South Korea and the space race, which at its height cost 4% of the GDP. The truth, rarely acknowledged, is that the USA has sponsored advanced science & technology and the national highway system but has called this Defence, the one form of expenditure that both liberals and conservatives could agree to and one that kills people. The end of the Cold War has brought with it, relative stagnation. Even the internet was bequeathed by government. Indeed, the US has by far the largest command economy in the world and a huge military industrial complex.

6. AND GIVING THE RESIDUE TO THE RAGING BULL WHO RE-INVESTS...

THE 'FEARLESS GIRL' STANDING UP TO THE 'RAGING BULL'.

The Raging Bull is a permanent feature in front of the New York Stock Exchange on Wall Street and represents a bull market raging to ever greater affluence with shares surging upwards. As of this time the exchange is still bullish, although the same cannot be said of Main Street, the US wage structure and the economy as a whole. We have no objection to shares climbing and investors being rewarded, provided this is not taken away from other stakeholders. Shareholders are entitled to the residue – what is left over, but what they typically get is a guaranteed advance, which those who do the actual work and the purchasing must pay for. The Fearless Girl is a much more recent addition. This is pre-pubescent child and she has not been granted a permanent place. The creator of the Raging Bull and backers have complained loudly that the addition of the girl has made the bull look menacing and this was never the intention. He threatens no one – much less a child. We believe that The Fearless Girl has to look out for her age cohort, heading for a generally bleak existence. She symbolizes the long-term view. But this is an opportunity to show just how successful patient investing can be. FoE stands for Firms of Endearment. Below we record the profits made by well-known companies who consciously bestow benefits on stakeholders.

FIRMS OF ENDEARMENT COMPARED TO S&P 500 AVERAGES

	5 Year	10 Year	15Year
Return Cumulative			
FoE	56.4%	254.4%	1646.1%
S&P 500	15.6%	30.7%	157.0%
Return Annualized			
FoE	9.4%	13.5%	21.0%
S&P 500	2.9%	2.7%	6.5%

The longer the period the better they do

b) HOW THE WEALTH-DESTRUCTION CYCLE WORKS

VICIOUS CIRCLE

You can't guarantee returns to shareholders in advance without siphoning off...

...monies due to other stakeholders whose productivity will consequently lag...

THE BROKEN BONDS RENDER THE CIRCLE VICIOUS

Companies are in the habit of planning in advance what their shareholders will receive. This is typically based on the previous year's operations with shareholders doing even better this year than last, where this is possible, since this is "progress" and we need to maximize their returns. All of this runs in the face of the economic orthodoxy which states that shareholders are entitled to the residue, what is left when all those with contracts have been paid what was promised to them. Shareholders are supposed to take the risk of being paid nothing unless that residue materializes and also to gain much if and when the residue is sizeable. What shareholders get should not be managed or guaranteed, but be the result of the company's skill and good fortune in the market-place. The profit will depend on how smartly and creatively employees have worked and how well and punctually suppliers have supplied. It will also depend on the degree of customer satisfaction and the revenue flowing from this. If you give the stakeholders a chance, pay them well, train them and elicit their innovation, there is no knowing by how much the company may grow and how well it might produce. We might be disappointed or hugely delighted, but we will not know until we have tried. Innovation is very uncertain in its outcome but it is certain to disappoint us unless we try. The bond between shareholders and stakeholders snaps. But if we guarantee shareholders in advance a certain share price and dividend and tell financial analysts about this, then it is likely that this will be taken away from employees, from suppliers, from customer satisfaction with quality, from health and safety and from training. What then happens is that their efforts and their engagement lag and the company generates less revenue not more. As the pie shrinks, activist shareholders will demand a larger share!

THE WEALTH-DESTROYING VICIOUS CIRCLE: SEGMENTS 1-6

THE BONDS BETWEEN STAKEHOLDERS HAVE SNAPPED.

Opposite we have illustrated a vicious circle to be compared with the virtuous circle described in the previous seven pages. This does not start with employees creating wealth which shareholders will collect to the extent that the former have succeeded, but by insuring shareholders will gain whatever happens. They will hardly be at risk at all since some of the monies previously paid to stakeholders will be siphoned off and given to shareholders instead. This is, of course, very unfair but it is also stupid, since monies paid to stakeholders motivate them to create the residue on which shareholders rely. If you cut back on production costs, on wages, and on R&D and make employees feel less secure and forced to produce more with fewer people, then their efforts will lag and their innovation will be far less, as many surveys show. Outsourcing to cheaper suppliers in Asia will destroy local supply-chains and the workers who once clustered in the vicinity will disperse for ever, impoverishing the region. Forcing suppliers to compete on price compromises quality. Paying them late is a forced loan and threatens survival. The broken ropes between the six segments symbolize that communication has been lost between shareholders and the five other stakeholders, most especially customers. Hence the Bank of Scotland put customers in special measures, not to help them survive, but to ensure they failed and their assets could be seized by the bank. As leaked e-mails put it, "give them enough rope to hang themselves." This reduces trust, poisons the community and harms the environment which is left to the government to clean up. Profits are not repatriated and re-invested, but hoarded in foreign tax-havens instead. Shareholders mobilize and pressure management into giving them a larger share...

1. **MORE MONEY FOR SHAREHOLDERS TARGETED BEFORE OPERATIONS START**

THE BIGGER BIRD GETS THE WORM.

Here we see the shareholders much better nourished than other stakeholders, getting the worm first before their skinnier companions in the nest. This is the wrong way around because it is their neglected stakeholders on which shareholders rely to run the business. Of all stakeholders it is the shareholders who are the most temporary and fickle, the most absent and far removed from the scene of action, the most ignorant of and unconcerned about those working in the company. It is rare for a shareholder to know day by day in what companies he or she is invested. Where risks are well-spread the shareholder may have as little as 0.5% of a share portfolio in a single company and to expect that person have much commitment is fanciful. There is likely to be a broker in any case. Most power is being given to the least committed. An employee may have given many years to the company. A supplier may have a shared fate with the success of his customer. The community may find its homes near worthless if a major employer quits. All are more engaged than shareholders who currently hold their shares for an average of five months! There is a notorious survey done by McKinsey & Company which found that most managers would cut back on R&D rather than miss the profit target they had been set. Since profits are reported quarterly and R&D may take 5-10 years to pay off, with the decision-maker long gone, it is hardly surprising that growth is so modest and the machine for making money is the order of the day. The long-term is being systematically sacrificed to the short-term by people who are less investors than traders. Nearly all the clever tactics for boosting share prices do not help the long-run and, in fact, actually harm it. This includes cutting wages, out-sourcing, deceiving customers and despoiling the environment, all dealt with in the pages that follow. It is the top managers with share-options who help themselves to the next spike. They have the inside information to gain whether they have succeeded or failed. An outside bid for their failing company may set them up for life! They can hardly go wrong!

2. And is wrested from staff via out-sourcing and cost-cutting

Contracts awarded to cheaper suppliers in East Asia.

What is the case for out-sourcing, for throwing contracts over the heads of your own one-time employees to foreign regions like China? It certainly helps the shareholders of single companies short-term. A 25% cut in the pay-roll costs can go straight into their pockets. No wonder announcements of redundancies make the price of shares rise. Workers may be fewer, harder-worked and more frightened but that will not show up for some time. Do they want to lose their jobs? Then there is the threat of out-sourcing which keeps unions and employees in line. But there are severe downsides as well. Outsourcing also collapses the ecosystem of smaller, local companies that once served you. They may disperse never to return. If you outsource hiring and selection to an outside contractor who has bid less than anyone else, do not expect to receive the best recruits. The contractor does not have the time. If you outsource to China, do not be surprised if they haul 600 million people out of poverty, while you face a famine of local skills. Do not be surprised if their people can buy more and your own people can buy less. If you send them all your blue-prints for components and your specifications do not wonder why they so easily catch you up.

When you outsource manufacturing you give away one of the most wealth-creating parts of the economy. Slower growth will be the consequence. Services rarely have the same order of productivity gains. It was C.P. Snow who warned us that "manufacturing is the last hope of the poor". If you outsource what they do, you are left with an angry, populist residue of hamburger flippers, on one third of their former salaries. Moreover, within an industrial eco-system, there are many groups of shareholders gaining at each other's expense and fighting over spoils. The problem with suppliers thousands of miles away and speaking another language is that it is much harder to relate to them creatively. You do not get to hear that a new solar cell could transform your solar panels and they can get this to you before anyone else, were you to invest in their plant…And of course, the lower your skill base, the sooner a robot will be able to take your job.

3. SUPPLIERS HAVE PRICES CUT, SCRIMP ON QUALITY, ARE PAID LATE & WILT

SUPPLIERS KEPT IN THEIR INFERIOR POSITION.

The cartoon opposite comes from a press report about a supplier who telephoned Tesco supermarket for a request. He was cut-off in mid-sentence and assuming the problem was technical he called back. But the problem was human. "When I speak, you jump," he was told. Of course, there are great differences in power between a large cash-rich retailer and the much smaller cash-poor suppliers whose very existence may hang on the account. The former can and do make the latter grovel. The question really is whether such bullying is not a gross folly. In the UK it is no secret that established companies may take 80 days or longer to pay bills, living off the credit of those who can least afford it to extend it. They do not hide the fact and even consider it a sign of privilege like the English gentleman who does not pay his tailor to remind of his inferior status. While clearly self-serving, it greatly weakens those who practice it. Small companies are the bed-rock of a successful economy, like Germany's three million Mittelstand. Gallup surveys have found that over 60% of Americans trust small business and less than half this trust big business. Small businesses are far more creative, grow faster, create more jobs and operate to human scale. Paying them late is too often a mortal blow. They may be profitable on paper but if they cannot pay employees or their bank on a particular day they die. Also destructive is getting suppliers to bid against each other and forcing down the price. What suffers is quality as companies desperate for a contract cut corners on health, safety, pension contributions and what can be hidden. If a first-tier supplier is paid eight months late, consider how the four lower tiers suffer! General Motors, under Ignacio Lopez de Arriortua clawed back $4 billion from dealers and suppliers, with Wall Street applauding- who cares for private companies? But, of course, the best of them had the last laugh. They did not have to put up with such conduct. It was GM who went bankrupt.

4. CUSTOMERS ARE OUTWITTED INTO BUYING BY CLEVER TACTICS

MUCH ADVERTISING CELEBRATES THE TRAILING EDGE OF TECHNOLOGY RATHER THAN THE LEADING EDGE.

Anglo-American capitalism seems near-addicted to targeting consumers as if this was some kind of sport like clay-pigeon shooting. There is a near irresistible urge to sell refrigerators to Eskimos not because they want or need them, but because it proves how persuasive you can be. Both countries do more consumer selling than B2B selling and the first of these has major flaws. The trouble with mass consumer advertising and marketing is that it exposes people with low commitment to what they are buying, to people with high commitment to what they are selling. Because the seller cares and the buyer cares far less, all manner of tricks and inducements are made to penetrate the unreflective minds of the uncommitted. The result is a culture of foaming nonsense; TV bringing to us the trailing, not leading, edge of capitalism, and hurling at us day after day a torrent of trivia and foolishness. The less the real difference between products, the more you need to stress an entirely spurious distinction, like coffee that is "re-heatable" and cereal that crackles and pops when milk is poured upon it. It is not enough to keep the mind alive! There are grown-ups advocating the "the breakfast with the built-in bounce," and testing it on people. The UK has a TV programme called *Rip Off Britain,* as if this was the most natural thing in the world and we should expect to be relentlessly bombarded with falsehoods. We were amazed when visiting China on how pervasive was the penetration of American fast-food outlets and how little the Chinese appear to have hit back with their own outlets. Then a nasty thought struck us; they are leaving saturated doughnuts and finger-sucking foods to us in our Hamburger Heaven, while they harness wind, sun and tides. For in the end, manipulating peoples' unexamined and unguarded habits is hard, exhausting, noisy, intrusive, expensive and largely without significance. It is less wicked than a colossal waste of time and energy, when we could be giving them what they need.

5...SO THAT TRUST, COMMUNITY AND SUSTAINABILITY ALL SUFFER...

POISONOUS RUBBISH IN OUR OCEANS.

It is in the interests of profit-maximizing shareholders to "take-make-waste", taking as much value as they can from the environment and dumping as much waste back as possible. Economists call this "externalizing" costs, with various stakeholders like community and government defined as outsiders. Plastic dumped in the ocean is merely the most recent threat. Eight million tons of plastic reach our oceans every year. This is equal to the weight of 26,000 Boeing 747s. There are huge garbage patches on the surface of our oceans swirling round and round. Five hundred marine species have been found with plastic inside them. Plastic does not degrade but breaks down in ever smaller particles and gets ingested. It has been found in sea creatures beneath many feet of polar ice. Much use of plastic is quite unnecessary – such as wrapping fresh foods in supermarkets, stiffening packages, bagging groceries and lining coffee cups. Vast amounts of money are wasted on trying to defeat regulations that hold businesses responsible and funds are given secretly for the rubbishing of climate research. Donald Trump recently withdrew from the Paris Climate Agreement hammered out among 180 nations.

Other forms of pollution are accidental, but here the cause is cutting back on safety. Such measures are rarely visible and require only inaction. Since shares are held for an average of months, the accidents when they come, will be someone else's loss. On the 20th of April 2010 at Deepwater Horizon in the Gulf of Mexico, BP and its contractor Haliburton caused the world's largest oil-spill, killing 11 workers. 4.9 million barrels polluted the Gulf. 2,200 tons of sludge washed up on Louisiana beaches alone. The company was fined $18.7 billion, the largest corporate settlement in history. No one was held criminally responsible.

6. PROFITS ARE SENT TO TAX HAVENS ABROAD, TAX AVOIDANCE PUSHED AND EVEN...

MONIES BURIED ABROAD TO SAVE ON TAXES.

John Maynard Keynes made the good point that money paid to a poor person would re-enter the economy in seconds, especially if s/he was hungry! But money paid to a rich person might well be squirreled away or used to buy influence. The whole point of making a profit is to re-invest it in new industries, new jobs and new ideas and/or to spend it so that demand rises. But this had not been happening. Entrepreneurship in the USA is actually down. Instead, the money is being moved to foreign tax jurisdictions and hidden and hoarded there. With current low interest rates, it is cheaper to borrow on your hidden money abroad than to bring it home and pay tax on it. Another trick is to offer to invest in poor countries abroad which have tax systems but demand a tax holiday, no health or safety regulations and no unions as a price for locating there and not somewhere else. This is a race to the bottom to see who can allow you to dump the interests of other stakeholders and do as little for that nation as possible while enjoying its low wages. Tax havens like Bermuda, Puerto Rico and the British Virgin Islands, either charge much lower income tax and capital gains tax than affluent nations, or no tax at all. They compete with each other in how little they charge and have little other industry but tax avoidance which creates no wealth at all, only money raised in other markets which are denied the revenue. The US has the highest corporate tax-rate in the world at 35%, but in respect to what the government actually receives, the rate is around the middle of the pack and riddled with loop-holes, amid thousands of pages of regulations. Corporate tax departments are seen as profit centres.   Yet this requires a whole army of lawyers willing to fight the government to a standstill and costing the nation dearly in expensive friction and litigation. Despite all this, shareholders are in general disappointed by the profits their exploited stakeholders have generated and numerous pension funds are in trouble. Shareholders demand a greater not a lesser share, as the vicious circle spirals downwards.

THE BONDS BETWEEN SHAREHOLDERS & STAKEHOLDERS HAVE SEVERED

Shareholder · Stakeholder

SHAREHOLDERS ARE CONCERNED WITH STAKEHOLDERS MERELY AS A SOURCE OF ENRICHMENT.

Here we have summarized the basic clash encountered in this section. The shareholder's greater power has been severed from the far lesser power of those with an actual stake in the company who produce the wealth we all need. The bargain is grossly uneven; "Here is some money, now give me your working life for as long as I want it." The employee, the supplier, the customer, the community, the purchaser and the environment are all subordinated to the shareholder and are producing and buying with declining enthusiasm and success. The top executives of the public company plus the CEO have share options and are on the side of the shareholders against those who actually create wealth and innovate. This palpable injustice greatly weakens the public company which is large and powerful but sadly sluggish and under-performing. Much of the present energy comes from private companies, who working as they do for the family, think long-term and are prepared to forgo high profits temporarily in order to prevail competitively. The success of the German Mittelstand and Asian dynastic companies are examples. Start-ups are also an important source of innovation, and much more innovative than larger companies, but get acquired by public companies and fail to renew themselves. We must give rewards to those who do the most outstanding work. Rewards do not motivate creative people as we have seen, since being innovative is its own reward, but they do facilitate innovation on a much larger scale and give recognition and high status to those skills and contributions we most need, so more people are prepared to do this vital work. We need real engineers, not financial engineers, people who want to be different, not those who want ever more of the same. When the rope snaps, communication breaks down and money fails to reach those with most to contribute to the economy and goes to those who feed our addiction to debt and junk foods.

Part III:

The Salience
of
Wicked Problems

THE SALIENCE OF WICKED PROBLEMS

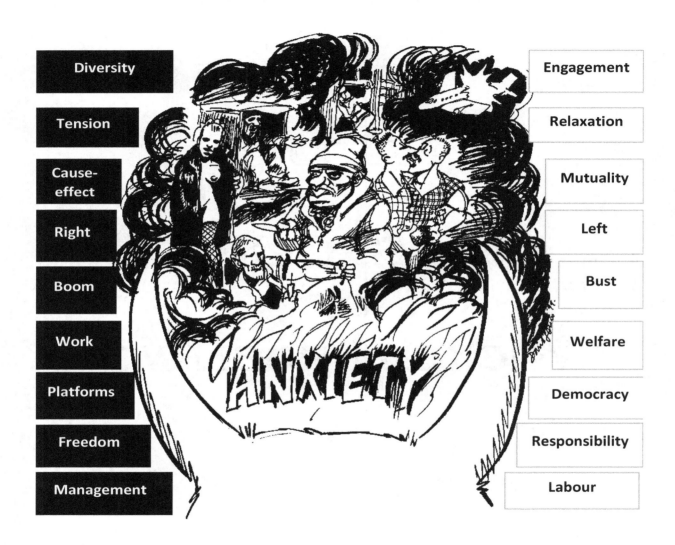

PROBLEMS THAT CONSTANTLY SURFACE AND DO NOT GO AWAY

What is a wicked problem? It is a problem that persists long-term and keeps on re-appearing, often in different guise. It grows out of defects in the way we think and conceive and it is we who perpetuate it time and again. As we globalize, we are forced to engage more and more people who are diverse in their experience of life, in their ethnic roots, in their sexual tastes, in their skin colour and in their religious and cultural beliefs, in their style of government. Engaging such people brings us vital knowledge but also a lot of ANXIETY (see picture). We have difficulty managing race relations and tend to avoid and/or dominate those who make us anxious, so that many then turn to crime in order to earn. We have difficulty managing our tension and turn to alcohol and drugs in our desperation to relax. We try to cause other people to behave in ways we think proper and so lose mutuality. The Right and Left in politics becomes ever more venomous and fixated on the sins of the other. Our economy lurches from boom to bust, irrationally exuberant then hopelessly depressed. Work and welfare become contradictory, curdling the milk of human kindness, our democracies are threatened by platform companies, management "triumphs" over labour, only to wreck the latter's purchasing power. Social media allows venomous personal attacks by people hiding their identity, thus severing freedom from responsibility.

DIVERSITY VS ENGAGEMENT: OPPORTUNITY AND DIRE THREAT

THOSE LIKE US BUT ALSO UNLIKE US, RAISE OUR ANXIETIES.

Are we betrayed by our anxiety? Supposedly rational human beings come up with extraordinary antics to keep anxiety at bay. When we encounter someone strange to us and are required to relate to them, our level of tension rises sharply. The dilemma we face is that these people are simultaneously like us in appearance having eyes, nose, mouth etc. but also unlike us, having different skin-colour, language and habits. There is no prejudice towards black cats and horses, because they are not like us at all, but someone like us behaving differently raises tensions in both parties to the encounter. (In mild forms tension become curiosity and excitement.) One expedient to reduce tension is to dominate the stranger, or to defer and "go native". The person who submits may be complicit in this arrangement. Another device is to avoid the stranger. When officially sanctioned, this is called apartheid or segregation. When not sanctioned, it takes the form of treating the person as invisible, or admitting "they all look the same to me". If that is so, it is because you have not looked at them hard enough or long enough to notice differences! Political correctness also controls anxiety by formulaic conduct. Because such tactics lower anxiety they get habitual. You do not really trust a stranger until you have relaxed in each other's presence. If you get tense and vigilant you will assume you were saved by your firearm & watchfulness. He would have attacked you but for your precaution! Then the tension will return. Diversity can bring us priceless insights and understanding AND it can trigger holocausts as we shall see.

TURNING DIFFUSE ANXIETY INTO SPECIFIC FEARS

turned to

PERSECUTING JEWS
LYNCHING BLACKS
PURGING "COMMUNISTS"
BURNING WITCHES
DISCOVERING "PAPISTS"
DEPORTING ALIENS

WE CAN 'TAKE CONTROL' AS THE BREXITEERS PUT IT, BY TURNING ANXIETY INTO FEAR OF SPECIFIC FOREIGNERS.

One of the persisting threats to civilization is turning vague, free-floating and pervasive anxiety which troubles so many of us, into a specific fear of selected scapegoats. There is nothing we can do individually about scarce jobs, about stagnant wages, about run-away inflation, about immigrants, about the possibilities of still-births, about approaching death. This is everywhere yet nowhere. It mantles us in a dread we cannot shake off. But if someone persuades us that a witch caused the still-birth and we burn her, then there is hope for the next pregnancy. If liberal policies have allowed conspiring communists to plot against America, if Jewish bankers cause inflation, if blacks lust after white southern womanhood, and that there is a Popish Plot against protestants, then anxiety about personal salvation can be turned into fear and hatred of specific people whom we can proceed to persecute and to punish. Low wages can be blamed on Mexican immigrants willing to work for less and taking away our opportunities. These immigrants should be barred entry by a wall or forcefully separated from their own children to punish the parents. Given the near-hysterical hatreds released by Brexit, the attack on judges, the threats of rape, murder and infanticide unleashed on female activists, anxiety is almost certainly at its roots. It was the least cosmopolitan areas who had voted for it, so the prospect of diversity not diversity itself was what triggered the reaction. Older people and poorer, less travelled people, were the most prone to oppose immigrants. They wanted to be "in control" of their own trepidation. The UK's economic decline was caused by foreigners so "keep them away from us".

SOME VALUE BIASES BEHIND BREXIT

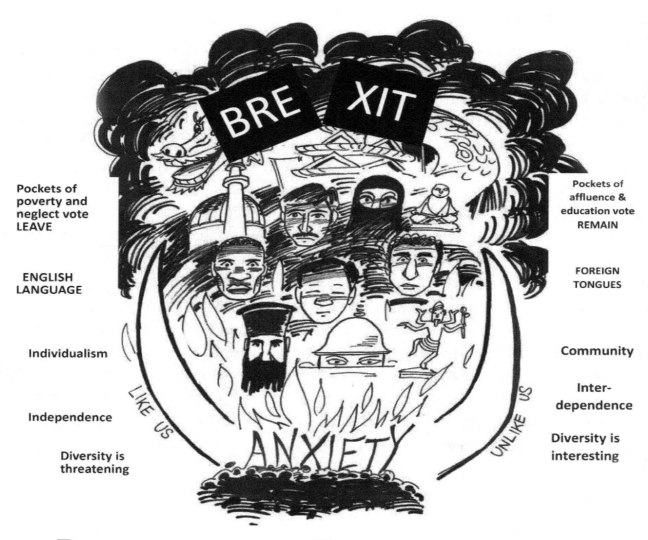

Pockets of poverty and neglect vote LEAVE

ENGLISH LANGUAGE

Individualism

Independence

Diversity is threatening

LIKE US

Pockets of affluence & education vote REMAIN

FOREIGN TONGUES

Community

Inter-dependence

Diversity is interesting

UNLIKE US

ANXIETY

BREXIT SCAPEGOATS EUROPE IN ITS GENERAL HOSTILITY TO WHAT IS UNFAMILIAR.

Brexit is a cultural revolt very much associated with anxiety. As Will Hutton and Andrew Adonis point out, in *Saving Britain: How We Must Change to Prosper in Europe,* in leave-voting Mansfield, in Nottingham, 71% of the electorate opted for Brexit, while in remain-voting Reading, 58% voted to remain. In Mansfield, wages are 19% below the national average and a large proportion of the population is on national benefits. In Reading, wages are 18% above the national average and a much smaller proportion are on benefits and those on benefits, receive over £1,000 less than those in Mansfield. This was true nation-wide - the poorer and the more neglected the community, the more likely it was to blame the EU and migrants for its plight, a classic case of scapegoating foreigners for Britain's neglect of its own pockets of poverty. Seven of the ten poorest are up north, others in coastal towns and their dilapidated hotels. But there are other cultural forces as well. The UK, with its many centuries of Common Law, is a law-giver and not a law-taker. The European Court of Justice is especially disliked. Britain hates that it has been an exception to the goal of greater unity within Europe, rather than a leader. It dislikes European diversity of tongue and habits and prefers the Anglosphere and those speaking the same language, (the USA, Canada, Australia, India and New Zealand) with whom trade pacts are anticipated. It wants less inter-dependence with other nations and more sterling independence reminiscent of its former imperialism. It dislikes the whole notion of a supra-national community of which the Queen and the English language are not the heads and insists on competing individualisms. It has little time for diffuse relations among cultures and understands what it can count; money, material things and people-as-units. The outer-direction involved in following European rules and directives is deeply resented, despite the fact that leaving cannot change this. The world's largest market will set rules which all corporations cannot afford to ignore! Britain is simply abdicating its influence. It teaches the world Economics despite its own deteriorating economic performance. It is true that immigrants take jobs but that is because training and skills development are so poor domestically. The more the actual experience of foreigners, as in London with its Muslim mayor Sadiq Khan, the more the wish to remain. The less the experience of foreigners, the greater is the phobic dread of them.

b) TENSION VS RELAXATION: THE ROOTS OF ADDICTION TO ALCOHOL

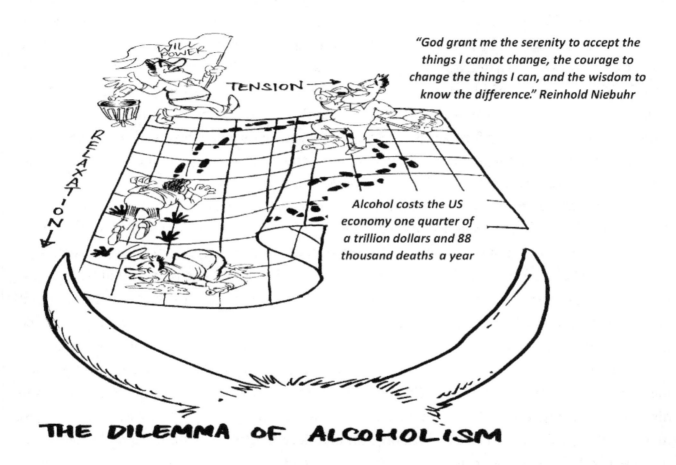

WILL POWER

TENSION →

RELAXATION

"God grant me the serenity to accept the things I cannot change, the courage to change the things I can, and the wisdom to know the difference." Reinhold Niebuhr

Alcohol costs the US economy one quarter of a trillion dollars and 88 thousand deaths a year

THE DILEMMA OF ALCOHOLISM

BY DRINKING, YOU DEMONSTRATE YOU ARE IN CONTROL AND STRONGER THAN THE BOTTLE.

We will look at one specific addiction and then ask what role an entire culture plays in addictions per se. Gregory Bateson studied alcoholics at the Veterans Administration Hospital, Palo Alto, California, nearly all male ex-soldiers. They showed remarkable unanimity in discussing their condition and its causes. Yet the way they thought was very much part of their problem. They all felt that they had too little will-power, that tempted by the Bottle they had yielded and that in future they should be stronger and not yield to temptation. Bateson's view is illustrated opposite. The alcoholic has chronically uneven values. He habitually manipulates other people and this makes him very tense and anxious (see the upper surface of the cusp catastrophe opposite). Others resent this so he forgoes the opportunity to relax in love and friendship with intimate others. Too much tension and too little relaxation are uncomfortable. However, alcohol is an artificial relaxant and when he imbibes he discovers just how desperate his body is to relax. He takes one drink and finds that he cannot stop such is his craving, and he drinks himself to collapse and "hits bottom". After his recovery he concludes that his strong Mind should have been in firmer control of his weak Body. As they say on US postage stamps, "Alcoholism, we can lick it." It only requires more manipulation! Indeed, dosing your body with alcohol is manipulation. You can abuse your partner and drown any regrets. We can now see why Alcoholics Anonymous beats most clinical practice. It forbids you to drink ever and gives you a friend to sit with till the craving passes so you relax with people. You must admit you are powerless against alcohol. You learn the Serenity Prayer (opposite). Bateson saw alcoholism as "flight from an insane premise", that your body is to be driven like a machine. But alcoholism is not the only high and low, the only rational manipulation and emotional crash in our culture. Many think their money, their gambling, drugs, sexual prowess and success will attract love. America is currently reeling from opioid addiction.

❧

c) Causation vs Mutuality: have we the wrong paradigm?

Should we even try to control other people?

The way we go about trying to solve problems in the social sciences is mistaken in the first place. Here we see another attempt by the scientist to emancipate people by formulae devised by him. He is the Independent Variable. They are the Dependent Variables dangling from his methodology. He will only get his PhD if he shows what pulling his strings has wrought, if he correctly predicts and controls. Were he to succeed, it would be all his doing and they would have done his bidding, not their own. All this is tragic nonsense and the ambition of social science to "war against poverty" and to cause another person's development is closer to a definition of the problem than of a solution. The method is oppressive in itself. Were it to succeed we would have enslaved ourselves. It could only end with the scientist more emphatically in charge than ever. $137 billion is the budget being recommended for the poverty industry, but is this wisely spent? That the subjects (objects) are ungrateful, rebellious, often corrupt, or effectively hang there helplessly is not altogether surprising. It is by no means clear what success would look like; a more orderly form of chronic dependence? To succeed you would have to dispense with the experimenter himself for a start! This ludicrous inequality dresses itself up as the Scientific Method, but all its hypotheses and calculations apply to people kept dangling from the structures of power. The truth is that we all want to be "independent" variables, but that being interdependent is probably better still. Micro-finance works by encouraging people to borrow manageable amounts and become independent variables themselves, honouring their promises to repay (mutuality). When they use a loan to produce more and then repay the bank from these proceeds they have taken their first step towards reciprocity and mutuality and away from dependence on others. To be poor is to have nothing to give, to have no freedom or discretion.

CAUSE-AND-EFFECT HATES MUTUALITY AND ASSAILS IT

A WIFE 'CONTROLLING' HER ERRANT HUSBAND.

It is no wonder that the social sciences teach us so little about love, understanding, mutuality dialogue and integrity. Their path to knowledge is via the attempt to cause another to behave as one wishes. Opposite, an angry woman is hurling a plate at her unfaithful spouse. We are not attacking her and defending him. She has much to be angry about. We are suggesting that cause-and-effect conduct is the antithesis of mutuality and essentially assails it. What makes her so angry is that she, not the other woman, has a right to married mutuality but has been denied it. Yet hurling a plate at the couple is unlikely to win it back. Do we not all want mutuality, rather than being targeted by irate persons? That the social sciences have brought us vast evidence of human pathologies of every kind is hardly surprising given the methodologies they customarily apply. That we discover so little of this in the "science" of what constitutes a good society, while studies of alienation, anomie and catastrophe abound, is not perhaps surprising. What is surprising is that experimenters claim to be "objective", when in fact they are measuring the impact of their own total domination, pitiless gaze and grim detachment. Approach someone with a clip-board and po-face and that is exactly what you will "discover". It is naïve to claim you did not elicit this reaction. The idea that someone controls and shapes another is abhorrent. It is not done well and we are surprised to see it even attempted. What are needed are relationships that will unleash the joy and the passions of partners – nothing else will suffice. We must grow each other and enterprise in general. What is it we want, to elicit the best from each other or to hurl the crockery? The desperation of social science to be "in control" is almost certainly a response to anxiety. If we let go this urge and let things happen to us, we would learn much more of mutuality.

FORTUNE MAGAZINE USED TO CELEBRATE AMERICA'S 10 TOUGHEST BOSSES

"Neutron Jack" (Welch) of GE was named after the Pentagon's neutron bomb that killed people but which spared property. He declared 112,000 managers redundant, closed 25 plants, and later dismissed 10% of all managers per annum, regardless of actual performance, to keep all frightened.

WHY SHOULD BOSSES BE TOUGH RATHER THAN TENDER?

The idea that CEOs command and control their organizations dies hard. For many years and well into the 90s *Fortune Magazine* extolled the year's Ten Toughest Bosses. Why it is virtuous to be tough rather than tender, understanding or participative has never been explained. The CEO is but one person, to elicit the energy, enthusiasm and engagement of thousands is almost certainly of greater value. That the organization is some kind of bulldozer that must run rough-shod over the needs and feelings of people is a very doubtful proposition indeed. The idea that people work better when frightened or threatened has been falsified so many times that we have lost count. It is oppressive but also very, very stupid and impacts very poorly on innovation and creativity. It helps to account for the domination of the male gender and helps to explain why the boss should get 350 times the median salary in the organization, which is no longer rare. "Toughness" towards employees sits well with shareholders. After all, he "causes" tens of thousands to excel by his direct orders. If the tough boss wants obedience he should get a dog or a computer. These are very much more reliable. Managers are paid for their discretion or degree of autonomy and the tough boss who is a "Loose Cannon", a "Cost Buster", a "Mega-Brain" or "Robespierre-on-a-rampage" as Fortune itself put it, comes from the world of Donald Trump and the nation's self-serving elite. That the West is now trailing other economies in wealth creation is not so surprising. The posture was and is, absurd.

d) Right vs Left - as stone statues on a deserted isle

THE NOTION THAT VALUES ARE THINGS LIKE THE ROCK OF AGES IS FALSE AND COULD DESTROY US.

P art of the problem with values and modern materialism is that we think of values as things set in stone and everlasting, rocks of ages. We take a left-wing/right-wing conflict like that between Equality, a state of fairness and justice in which every person is judged to be as good as others and the value of Excellence, whose money-making virtue is supposed to trickle down to the rest of us. We polarize the two. Equality is seen as wrecking the ideal of Excellence by obscuring talent. Those espousing Excellence are seen as relegating large swathes of humanity to subordination. Each side throws rocks of rectitude at effigies of the opposed value. But suppose values are not like rocks at all, but more like ripples on a pond. Suppose Equality especially, is less an effigy and more a PROCESS, so that innumerable varieties of people are treated as equals in the process of discovering at what they are most excellent. Human attainments are very wide and very varied. To treat others as equals is a process of discovery. They may indeed be inferior to you in this respect and that, but you need to treat them as an equal to find this out! Equality is an expectation which in part fulfils itself. Treat the others as equals and they grow before your eyes and give to you the best of their capacities. Everyone deserves an equality of opportunity to excel. Excelling is a process too and in relationships of equality we discover just how much each of us can learn and develop. The inhabitants of Easter Island built stone statues like those opposite, cutting down all of their trees to move them. The statues are there to this day – only the people died out. In parts of the West so great is the vitriol and name-calling that democracy itself is in danger, corrupted by eager hackers, who under the cloak of anonymity can discharge their own despair and bile. Left and right properly seen are a synthesis and an integrity, with equality eliciting excellence from the many.

Left vs. Right in politics as a wicked problem

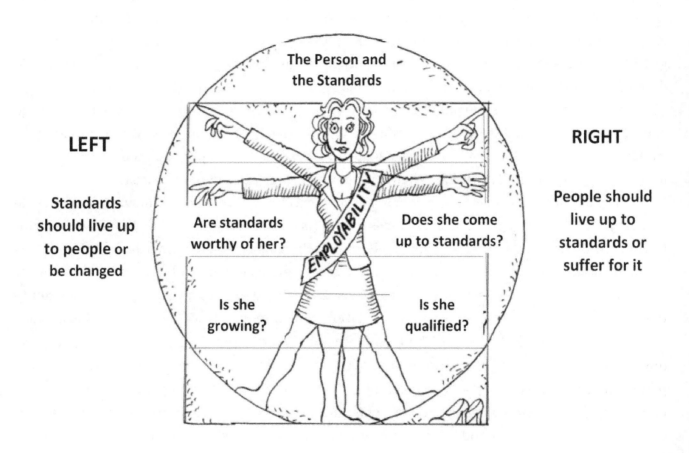

LEFT

Standards should live up to people or be changed

The Person and the Standards

Are standards worthy of her?

Does she come up to standards?

EMPLOYABILITY

Is she growing?

Is she qualified?

RIGHT

People should live up to standards or suffer for it

SHARE MY WORK ETHIC, NOT MY WEALTH.

The battle between left and right is typical of a wicked problem. It never goes away, both left-wings and right wings have policies that prove unsatisfactory and the polarization itself is full of emotion and rancour. When nations compromise as they must, both wings feel cheated and impure. In the image opposite, the person is pictured surrounded by various measures of virtue. We take our definition from Silvan Tomkins. The Left believes "Man (or woman as opposite) is the measure, the end in herself, an active, creative, thinking desiring, loving force in nature." The Right believes, "Woman must realize herself, attain her full stature only through struggle towards, participation in and conformity to, a norm, a measure, an ideal essence basically independent of her." This difference runs through a whole gamut of issues. A person should be free to define their own sexuality/gender (Left). A person should be normal, heterosexual and stick with the gender they were born with (Right). No person should be left behind in poverty (Left). People who do not make sufficient efforts to earn have only themselves to blame (Right). People must be allowed to express themselves and grow (Left). People should not be allowed to express ideas that undermine correct standards (Right). You are good if you come up with original ideas (Left). You are good if come up to Christian, Jewish, Muslim, Hindu standards (Right). This even takes place in disciplines. "Mathematics is the finest form of human play" (Left) versus "Only under this discipline can the human mind achieve results of scientific value" (Right). In the US Supreme Court, the members ask "Does this seem to us fair?" (Left) or "What does the Constitution say on this matter?" (Right) This split is totally unnecessary as the banner on the woman explains. We cannot offer her life-long employment because of rapid technological change and the replacement of one standard by another, but we can render her more employable within that industrial eco-system. We can leave her better off via employment. You descend the stairs of your own volition (Left) but brush the banister with one hand lest you stumble (Right). Moral leaders like Gandhi and Martin Luther King accepted jail to show they were not against laws in general, only specific discriminatory laws. They reconciled Right and Left.

e) Boom vs Bust: are we addicted to boom and bust?

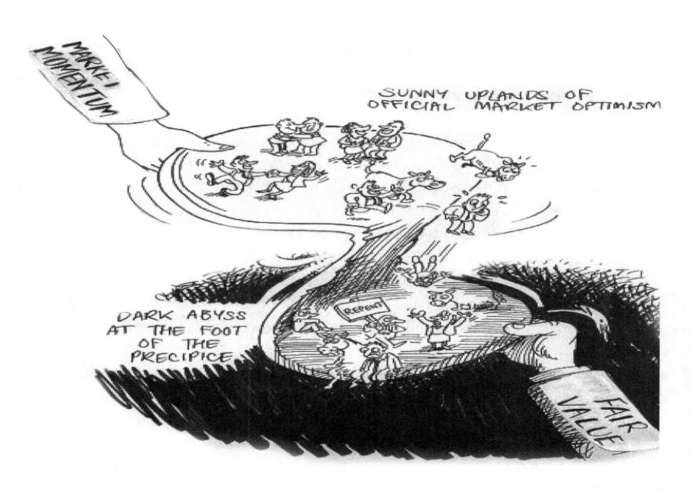

INVESTORS CAUGHT IN CUSP-CATASTROPHE. ECONOMIC MAN AS AN EMOTIONAL WRECK.

A lot of financial analysts work hard on assessing "the fair value" of a particular company. Where the stock price goes above their estimate of fair value, they advise clients to sell. Where it falls below this estimate, they advise clients to buy. So long as markets are tranquil such estimates work well and the analysts earn their money. But major problems arise when you have a boom and the whole industry has momentum and surges upwards. This occurs from time to time as during the Dot-Com boom at the beginning of this century which crashed in a spectacular manner, as did the housing bubble in 2007-8. When the share price runs ahead of your fair value estimate what do you do? You are pretty sure a crash is coming but you do not know when. If you counsel to "sell" your clients will miss out on further share appreciation and may get angry with you. They sold while others bought and the others are now ahead. Quite a few analysts lost their jobs by warning the Dot-Com boom would crash and that disaster was imminent. You may also be accused of triggering the fall if you state too emphatically that shares are over-priced. Markets like optimism, that way booms last longer. What routinely happens is that a huge gap opens up between Momentum on the left and Fair Value on the right. Everyone is getting jumpy. This is too good to be true! They smile for public consumption on the outside and quake with anxiety and dread on the inside. The smallest incident may trigger a correction which becomes a stampede and then a cusp catastrophe. The sunny uplands yield to the dark abyss as the stock plunges down. Volatility haunts the market and is never far away. Despite economics being super-rational, our so-called animal spirits get the best of us and we seem condemned indefinitely to Boom and Bust, trapped between greed and fear and desperately speculating on other people's states of mind. When all is said and done, Economic Man is an emotional wreck.

THOSE WITHIN THE FAULTY SYSTEM EXPLOIT IT TO OUR DETRIMENT

ECONOMIC CATASTROPHE AS A CHANCE TO SELL SHORT.

We need to stop a system which is flawed from being exploited by those in it. When a financial bubble forms you know it will burst, since say – house prices are rising four times faster than incomes – but you do not know when this will occur. It is in the interests of those chasing the bubble to keep chasing it and get out just in time as it reaches its peak. It is also in their interests to "short" the whole process of the boom, that is to spend their clients' money in extending the boom as long as possible and spending their own money in betting that asset prices will collapse. That way you gain whatever happens. You gain on the upside of the boom and also on the downside. You also do nothing to stop the boom and bust from occurring since you make money from this process and the only loser is the real economy and ordinary people. As the film *The Big Short* showed, the peril to the nation and much of the world is seen as an opportunity for private gain at the expense of populations. Indeed, you deliberately run the economy over the edge to deepen its collapse and you sell financial products which are hedges against the very volatility you encouraged in the first place. Collapses are sudden and catastrophic, because many have been privately expecting it while publicly extolling the boom. It is important to grasp that such speculation makes a lot of money but creates no wealth. In such speculative markets, gains for some exactly match losses for others. The society is no better off. Indeed, the volatility is bad for business in general and the financial sector gains at the expense of the larger economy. The smartest people do not warn us of what is coming; they gain at the expense of the public.

TRAPPED BETWEEN VERY LOW WAGES AND NO JOB AT ALL.

Welfare is a very curious system. It sits side by side with the casual labour market but is a total contradiction to earning your way in the world. It is also extremely expensive for tax-payers and the nation, and those on welfare are widely despised. It is very hard for an impoverished person to join the work-force. S/he may be offered a zero-hour contract that endangers welfare entitlement without guaranteeing any money at all! You can wait all day to be called. Even if you get work it is likely to be of brief duration because employers seek to avoid social security payments and it is cheaper to hire someone else instead very briefly. Getting back on welfare is then difficult and worrying. So much so that switching between begging and bargaining is very painful for the individual. As illustrated opposite he is never quite good enough for work nor quite wretched enough for the welfare system. Any attempt at self-help is treated as an abuse of the welfare system that demands you be hopeless and helpless, beyond all doubt; to earn on the side is to "cheat". In truth, welfare was never designed as a way of life, it was there to tide you over between jobs. Once it becomes a way of life, breeding dependent children to collect a livelihood, it becomes palpably absurd. We pay people for doing nothing and their idleness is a pre-condition for that payment. The "job-seekers allowance" is a very flimsy bridge between the upper and the nether millstones between which the victim is ground. It is not too difficult to look for work without getting it and even where you get it, how long can it last? If Satan were asked to invent a system to keep the body live but break the spirit, we doubt he could do better; a system of endless torture for all involved, a bureaucratic marketing board for the milk of human kindness, that is so hated by recipients that staff are in fear of assault and police hover nearby. To be a taker and never a giver erodes human morale. One bright spot is that any other systems would be an improvement and to showing how the poor could organize themselves, as we explain in volume 2.

g) Cambridge Analytica: the problem with data mining

Communication is corrupted when it deliberately appeals to known prejudices.

The word data is Latin for "things given". Our minds it seems are full of things and objects and it is the concern of the advertising industry what additional things and objects we can be induced to buy. The chief problem with this is that data are dead and morbid in their influence. What generates life is the vital organization of elements, what Socrates called the soul. A few seconds after our deaths the chemical composition of our bodies is no different. What has failed is the integrity of the whole, the relationship among the elements. "Our meddling intellect mis-shapes the beauteous form of things and murder to dissect," In order to get data you have to hack into mental connections like a coal-face and bring the debris to the surface. Courage is hacked off from Caution to bring us the reckless and the cowardly, the shattered value continuum. Self-interest is severed from concern for others to bring us selfishness and tribalism, as shattered pieces. Disconnected values are all vices by definition, the obsessions, the fetishes, the female body parts, the pet hates, the lying statistics, the loose, disowned, shameful pieces and prejudices that rattle around inside us and that we dare not show to friends and family. But we can and do reveals these skeletons to fellow addicts and become immensely grateful that there are others out there who are shoe-fetishists or collect child pornography. People with loose screws inside them have a fierce confirmation bias. They seek out other anti-Semites or immigrant-haters and bask in their approval. When we know enough about such voters according to Christopher Wylie, the whistle-blower from Cambridge Analytica, we can whisper in their ears. Hillary Clinton is a secret exponent of a foul mutation, a transgender conspiracy. Why did CA finish up working for the alternative Right and sundry strong men? Because finding out what people already believe and reinforcing pet hatreds is highly reactionary and encourages existing extremism, a triumph of Trumpery. It renders all progress nearly impossible and fills the body politic with secret, rumoured terrors.

PLATFORM COMPANIES CAN OVERPOWER WHOLE NATIONS.

FAKE NEWS SPREADS FAR FASTER. GIVE THEM WHAT THEY LONG TO HEAR.

Platform companies like Facebook which recently allowed nearly 90 million American voters to have their voting information hacked, Google, Twitter, WhatsApp, Uber and Airbnb are potential threats to our democracy according to Jamie Bartlett, author of *The People vs. Tech*. Is this alarmism? He cites the fact that while we connect with people, we actually get further apart from them. These are people we do not genuinely know – they may not even exist in the form they present to us – yet we share guilty secrets with them. Because we cannot actually see the hurt we cause in their faces, the media are full of hatred, bullying, threats and abuse. Ask any female member of Parliament; they have all been threatened with unspeakable crimes. The Internet has become a spittoon for ranting diatribes. Suicides and self-harm are on the rise. Time owed to the family is spent on hounding the scapegoats of our discontent. These are technologies that senators seem to know all too little, judging by naïve questions to Mark Zuckerberg. "Project Alamo" was named after the resistance to the Mexican army, and its "bull pen" of "hackers", (metaphors in use tells you much about the culture of this Pro-Trump organization). They were armed by 5,000 data points for some 230 million Americans all considered as "targets" for round-the-clock "hits", an "information war" in which truth was the first casualty. "The data drove the content." In short, people were told things they already believed and wanted to hear and told to re-tweet them to like-minded colleagues. Bartlett sees us as suffering from information overload and desperately needing coherence so that telling us what we already believe is felt as a blessed relief, a small island of reassurance. But it kills public debate on shared issues to have private hang-ups secretly and anonymously sent. These platforms are in many cases global, much larger than national political constituencies and with vast amounts of money to lavish on legislators. Internet ad revenues are closing newspapers and slowly killing investigative journalism and informed debate. Private, customized messages are uncheckable and full of lies, while personality profiles check for "openness" or rather credulity. When Bartlett interviewed Alexander Nix of CA, *Stealing Elections* was boldly on display, as was *The Bad Boys of Brexit*. These are people who exult in their subterfuge, boast that their e-mails destroy themselves and that Ukrainian prostitutes can compromise the political rivals of their clients.

H) Freedom vs Responsibility: anonymity strips responsibility away from freedom

Secret identities spawn poisonous messages.

We are not aware of a case of the Ku Klux Klan messing electronically with black children. The point we are making, is that attempts to communicate while hiding your identity end in gross inequality and palpable harm to the deceived, to the extent that the internet permits communication from persons who hide their identities and takes no personal responsibility for what they are saying. The results will be pathological and socially disastrous, in the manner of poison pen letters, black balling etc. Suicide and self-harm are becoming epidemic and mental health is deteriorating. Societies survive through civil conversations between intimates who own their words. A group of bullies baiting a child anonymously is the responsibility of the owner of the technology being used. There are no technical systems without accompanying disturbances to the social systems of those using them. A gun is not "as good or bad as the person using it." It is a form of extreme prejudice in which those who fire first are likely to kill any less reckless opponent. A moment's pause to question what you are doing can prove fatal to your survival. An armed confrontation makes bigots of us all. Similarly, forms of electronic communication where you can groom an innocent child without saying who you are is not a neutral instrument but an open invitation to corrupt and oppress. All users should register their real names and use them. All those using deception to oppress should be exposed for who they are. At least the Klansman is known to hide his identity. On the internet we cannot tell a teenage buddy from a drooling septuagenarian begging pictures of children's private parts.

MANAGEMENT VS LABOUR: THE BOAT GROWING MORE UNSTEADY

Two sets of sailors trying to steady a boat that was steady to begin with

ADVERSARIAL RELATIONS CAN BE A LUDICROUS WASTE OF ENERGY.

The image and phrase quoted opposite is from the work of Paul Watzlawick. The further one partner leans out to the left, the further the other side must lean out to the right if the ship is not to capsize in either direction. Neither side is being irrational and both fear that if they moved closer to the mast, the other side would exploit them and sink the vessel. They dare not let this happen. But these rational calculations do between them produce a result both irrational and absurd with all concerned living with their behinds in the water. It is clear from the picture opposite that management is winning or has "won" the labour relations battle in the USA and UK. Labour unions are greatly weakened and are in decline. Indeed, manufacturing which used to employ most unionized workers, is down to 10% of the UK economy and 11% of the US economy. Mrs. Thatcher won the coal strike but lost the whole industry in the process. Labour's loss of bargaining power has caused wages to stagnate for a whole generation and has chronically lowered consumer demand in both countries so that industry slows - some victory!

Other countries seem to be able to relate to their manual workers with far less trouble and one reason for so much outsourcing is that some nations manage their people more reliably and deliver on time. But manufacturing is a major source of added value and of high wages. Both economies have suffered severely from its decline. It seems you lose by winning. The American South with its right-to-work laws remains poorer than the North. The reasons for bad labour relations are in part historical. Both countries industrialized early and when rivals began to catch them tried to reduce wages, a tactic that enraged workers who were producing more than ever. The adversary nature of labour relations makes for poor productivity, especially in the UK. It arguably created communism which held that the proletariat would assume dictatorial powers before the state withered away. We only needed the two sides of industry to share one fate between them.

⸺

Part IV

Mind-set, Re-set:

Learning to think differently

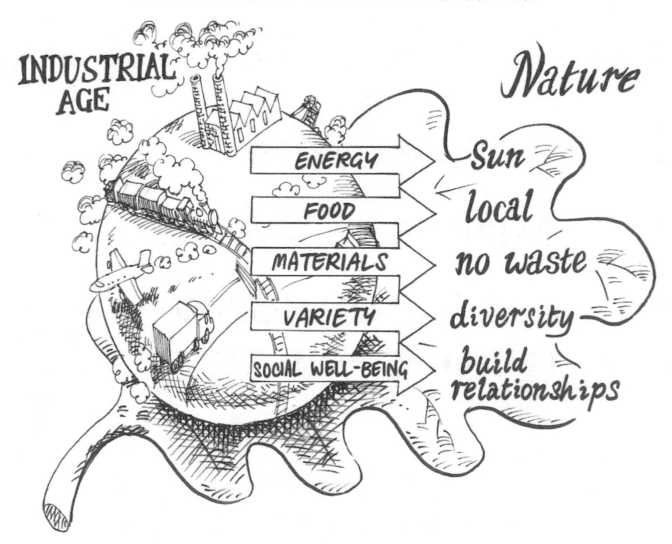

HOW INDUSTRY IS CHANGING.

We are passing out of the Industrial Age into the Age of Nature. We will not here rehearse the arguments about how great is the threat from global warming, plastic debris, ozone depletion and so on. Given the chance of working with the earth's natural forces or against them and given the fact that sun, wind and tides are free, the answers are surely obvious. We are part of a living whole or we are dead. This part of the book we call Mind-set-Re-set because we must learn to think like living systems, not like machines calculating forcefulness. At its heart, nature is circular, systemic, paradoxical and fractal and so must be the way we think about our only habitat. Our societies have been socially constructed so that its successes and failures lie within our basic assumptions. This section will argue a) the economy is not a machine-in-sky, b) How we think decides the social reality we construct. c) What it means to be alive. d) Living systems and the economy are circular. e) At the heart of nature is paradox. f) Concern for the whole eco-system must precede its parts. Among other things we will contend that we are all in search of larger meanings. Only stakeholders working together in all their variety and diversity can bring this about. We must learn to sustain the Nature which sustains us. The unit of survival is not man alone but our relationships with the environment. How finely can we fit? Can we learn to bless the earth that blesses us?

A) # THE ECONOMY IS NOT A GOD-LIKE MACHINE IN THE SKY

WHY NOT A MARKET ORGANISM?

The Free Market is very much a "Machine in the Sky", an absentee Protestant deity that rewards prudence and effort and punishes extravagance and sloth. It is impersonal like the unoccupied crucifix and the Word of God written in the scriptures on a printed page. Why it should be a machine, rather than a lotus flower, a tree or an organism is hard to say. Economics was invented in the Machine Age and borrowed the most prominent industrial metaphor of its time. Besides, a machine is impersonal. That a machine is also dead might be considered a handicap. It was widely understood that the universe was similar to a celestial clock which God had wound up and set in motion, only to absent Himself. He did not intervene miraculously in human affairs, as Roman Catholics believed. He left his clock to tick on by itself. If you wanted to worship God then working out how the clock functioned was a sacred calling. Many of the early Puritans were also scientists. It was holy work to study the machine. This accounts for how quickly science became secularized in Britain and the USA. The machine is in automatic equilibrium and despite the cut and thrust of commerce, returns to a steady state of supply and demand. If we 'leave it to the market' anomalies will right themselves over time. Interference in this ideal balance is akin to blasphemy. To let the markets decide, is to surrender to a Higher Will than our own. Our salvation comes from working humbly on the messages the market sends us, while the clock with its Invisible Hand converts this into public benefit. The view taken here is that the market is at times a useful servant, but a poor master and a worse object of veneration. How and when it succeeds and fails is to be discovered. The market is not an "it" but rather "us", with all our failings, excesses and misconceptions. It is a turmoil of ideas and artefacts to which we must be free to contribute but whose equilibrium is very much in doubt and is continually punctuated by upheaval verging on chaos.

B) WHAT IT MEANS TO BE ALIVE: THE VITALITY OF THE WHOLE

Economics is a mature, rational, mathematical science of machine-like efficiency and equilibrium

The economy is prey to irrational exuberance and panics together with chronic disequilibrium

With clever financial analysis everything is reducible to small specific pieces.

Only creative synthesis generates wealth. The whole has meanings absent in the parts.

WHOLES HAVE A CHARACTER THAT PARTS LACK.

What does it mean to be alive? For a few minutes after we die the composition of our bodies is very much the same. All the bits and pieces are there. What has broken down is the body's organization. It no longer functions as a live whole. It follows that to be a living whole is to be more than the sum of our parts. The animating principle must be present and if absent, we are not alive in any sense. We consider here whether economics, with its theory of the person as a covetous, rational machine, really respects the principles of human life in any degree. The image at the top shows economics as it likes to portray itself, as a codified science of rational, mathematical, calculated decision-making. The reality is very different. After intervals of relative calm, it goes into periodic bouts of boom and bust, like a wave crashing down in turmoil and thousands of people lose any semblance of the reason to which they once laid claim, as heady exuberance gives way to panic. If you repress emotion it returns to haunt you. The image at the bottom shows the limitations of the analytic approach which reduces everything to bits and pieces. When we are dismembered we are no longer human. The pieces do not explain the whole and when we sever human relationships in the process of analysing, we miss what actually creates wealth. Creativity, synthesis and meaning rely on the quality of the combinations we have wrought. They are not present in the parts of the puzzle, only in the living whole. If indeed people work for meaning, then when analysts are through, meaning is in very short supply. We need superordinate goals and good reasons for developing each other.

WHAT IT MEANS TO BE ALIVE: MUTUALITY NOT CAUSE-AND-EFFECT

Half-Truth 3

Individuals can and do make money and "score goals" by sovereign will-power.

Larger Truth 3

Unilateral manipulation and leverage comes full circle as our own toxicity lashes back at us.

Mutuality is the secret of effective human relationship

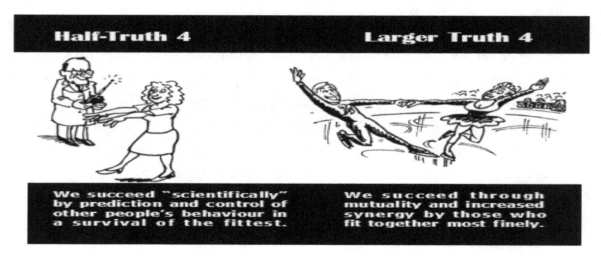

Half-Truth 4

We succeed "scientifically" by prediction and control of other people's behaviour in a survival of the fittest.

Larger Truth 4

We succeed through mutuality and increased synergy by those who fit together most finely.

MUTUALITY IS THE SECRET OF RELATIONSHIPS

It is sheer nonsense to claim that one human being "causes" another living creature to behave in a particular way. In their eagerness to be like the hard sciences (physics envy), many social scientists have assumed that we can impact on a live creature much as a boot impacts upon a football. This is fine so long as the object is dead. But if it is not a dead piece of leather but a live pit-bull, then kicking it at it is going to occasion a nasty surprise. Note that the dog's reaction to being kicked comes full circle, while the footballer envisages a straight line. This is one more reason for advocating circular reasoning as we have, elsewhere in the book. The reason for this is obvious. All living creatures have nervous systems with particular predispositions apart from our own, one of which is not being kicked. If we assault another nervous system it will turn on us. We do not "cause" a creature to respond to us, we trigger a response by what we do or say and that creature can be expected to advance its own agenda. We may teach it tricks but it gets better fed that way! The dream of having total unilateral control, see bottom left, is fortunately not possible but it requires subordination and deceit even to attempt this, as in experiments in obedience and conformity by Stanley Milgram, largely contrived by lying to subjects. What develops people is harmony and synergy between them and their skills, symbolized by the dance on ice (bottom right). Each nervous system is in tune with the other and together they create an aesthetic performance from what they have learned and which the audience appreciates and pays to watch. This is wealth-creation.

AN ECONOMY CAN BE LIKE A TREE WHICH WASTES NOTHING

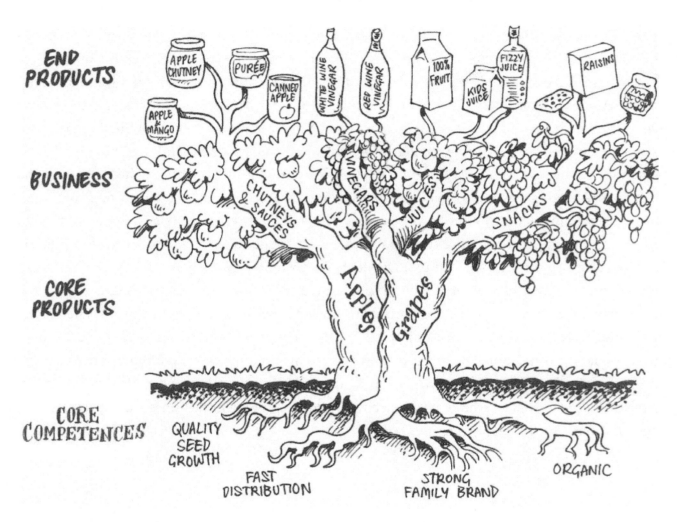

AN ENTERPRISE IS A LIVING WHOLE, NOT BITS OF MACHINERY.

Instead of conceiving of the economy as a machine bulldozing the environment or chain-sawing forests, why do we not think of it as a tree? A tree has the virtue of being alive, of creating the oxygen without which we could not survive; moreover, a tree wastes nothing while sustaining the environment. Its falling leaves enrich the ground, its blossoms engage the eye, its fruits sustain animals. It grows new trees and provides wood. It anchors the soil and captures sun and rain. In the illustration opposite, Gary Hamel and C.K. Prahalad have likened a corporation to a tree. Its core competences are the roots of its growth, i.e. seed quality, fast distribution and a strong family brand. It uses apples and grapes as its core products, turning these into chutneys and sauces, vinegars, juices and snacks. From these five businesses it produces a large variety of end products illustrated at the summit of the picture. Note that while there is great variety in what is offered to the market, there is unity among sources from which it comes, apples and grapes; the better and the more economically these are grown the more wealth is created. The company must develop its core competences to a level which no other company can match and then offer the fruits of these to the market at large with all its variance. A tree makes a very much better metaphor for creating wealth than does a machine with its severely limited series of operations and often destructive forces. A tree is to be treasured, nurtured, pruned, grown and harvested. A tree has a benign interaction with its environment and makes a habitat for many other insects and creatures. Trees are among evolution's greatest feats of endurance and sustainability, a lesson to us all. When they cut the trees down on Easter Island to shift their stone effigies, all life perished, only stones remained.

THINKING IN DEPTH SYSTEMICALLY

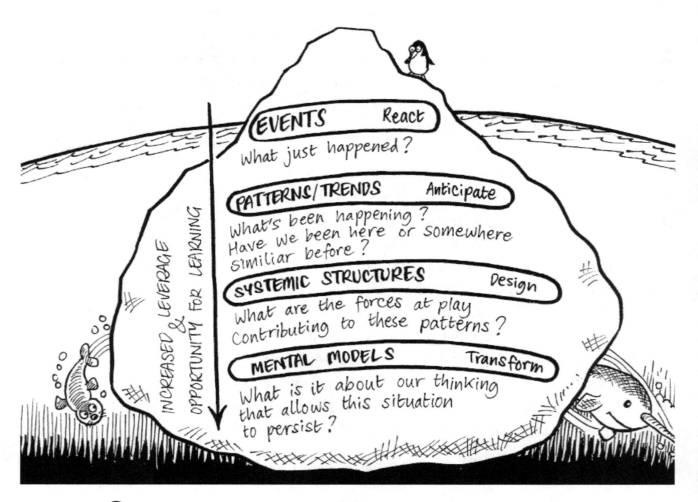

CAN WE LEARN TO PERCEIVE PATTERNS, SYSTEMS AND WHOLES?

The illustration opposite comes from the work of Peter Senge. We pride ourselves in the West of being empiricists, looking at "events" and "facts". This is correct up to a point insofar as explanations need to account for facts and events otherwise they fail us. But events are on the surface and quite superficial. They also throw us into turmoil as did the recession of 2008. For this reason, we go beyond events to look at patterns. Is there something about markets we have not grasped? Have the Russians murdered exiles in the UK before? But this is not nearly deep enough. What are the systemic structures lying beneath these patterns? Why have thousands of drug raids done nothing to stem the trade? Is it because the raids raise the price of drugs and the drug system restores itself and profits even more? Is it, as this book argues, that capitalism as a system is in some ways defective? None of this can be tackled unless we examine our own mental models, the deepest layer in the illustration, which have shaped the systems underlying these patterns. The very fact that we take events so seriously comes in part from the way we see the world, as particles not waves, parts not wholes, as an earth to be dominated not nurtured and sustained. If we seek to make fundamental changes to our culture then we need to re-examine what many of us have taken for granted much of our lives. Cultures have deeply embedded assumptions and some are more favourable to creating wealth and to innovating than are others. In order really to learn, we cannot just ask ourselves "does this person come up to scratch?" We need to ask "does scratch come up to the endowment of human beings? Should the model itself be changed?"

c) ADAM SMITH AND THE PHANTOM CIRCULAR HAND

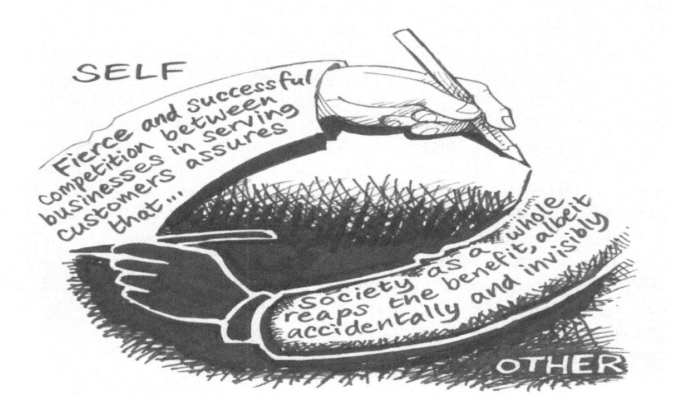

THE INVISIBLE HAND

SELF

Fierce and successful competition between businesses in serving customers assures that...

Society as a whole reaps the benefit, albeit accidentally and invisibly

OTHER

WHY ONE HAND AND NOT TWO?

Adam Smith's brilliant insight was to see that wealth creation was circular and combined two very different values in a powerful combination. Where merchants competed with one another in serving customers, the more successful would win and those customers and the wider society would be well served by this combination. It was only necessary for the merchants to pursue their own interests and make rational economic decisions to their own advantage, and the public good would benefit as it were by an Invisible Hand. And the fiercer the competition, the greater the subsequent benefit bestowed on society in general. There was no need for moderation; only the most competitive moves would suffice. Those like Smith's aristocratic boss, whose son Smith tutored, claimed to "serve the public good". Smith was the spokesperson for the rising bourgeois class, even then challenging the landed aristocracy. He saw their "service" to the nation as mere privilege. We are all out for ourselves and should not pretend otherwise. There was a healthy dose of reality in what Smith claimed and in the context of his day it was liberating. But is it good enough for our present day? Why do our motives need to be singular? When baking bread at dawn why not think about what customers most liked the day before? When banking the proceeds why not think of your own advantage? One motive does not need to obviate the other. Because Smith thought in terms of cause and effect he had to claim that self-interest caused customer benefit. But does it not work the other way around? Might sympathy and liking for customers and the desire to serve them "cause" self-interest to be served? We are all customers! Or maybe cause is the wrong word, we have a circular system with two contrasting values spurring each other in harmony. Smith was just half-right.

Markets are also circular: the baker

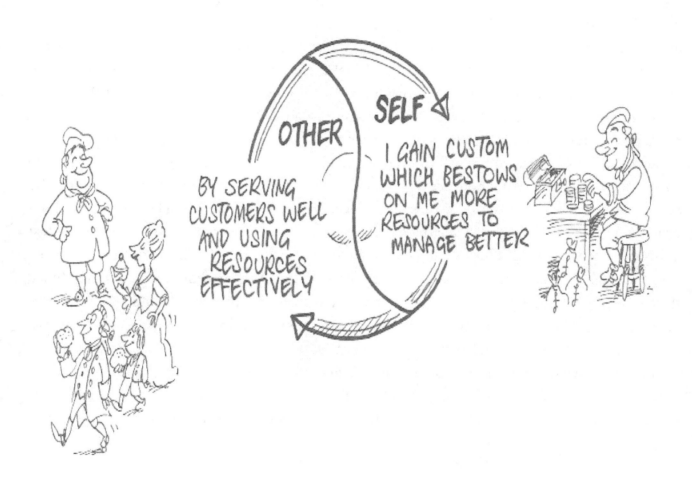

We actually profit indirectly.

Adam Smith liked to cite butchers, bakers and brewers in his examples of businesses motivated by self-interest. Even if we accept his premise that we are all driven primarily by the desire for gain, and in this book we do not, there remains the stubborn fact that by looking after customers and pleasing them, the supplier gains their revenue. Satisfying customers must come first in time and the gain for the baker is but subsequent. Whether or not he cares about anyone else but himself, serving others must take precedence. In Smith's day most people lived in small towns and villages and it was hardly possible to avoid your customers. They would crowd your shop every day and if there were only two or three bakers their verdict would be decisive. Much of your social life and the reputation of your family depended on what they thought of your wares. Note that the better he serves customers the more will be his gains and the more he is able to plough profits back into even better provision. He will get more resources to manage even more effectively. He does not open fire on his customers; he feeds them and the service is the pre-condition of his own economic survival. Note also that additional resources from customers in the shape of more revenue will move towards the best baker and away from any less skilled competitors. In that sense the market rewards skill and higher quality and punishes the lack of good provision and we can expect the baking of bread to improve as a craft over time due to these pressures. Note also that Smith uses the "public interest" as a straw man. Of course, the local brewer or baker does not concern himself with anything so abstract and grandiose and of course they do not pontificate about it. But if we are concerned with self and other, the customers are the day-to-day manifestation of the Other, not the public interest. In Smith's world the others were both numerous and pressing. In the face-to-face conditions then prevailing, you could not pursue your self-interest without encountering those who made this possible by their patronage.

HERE IS HOW THE MARKET IS SUPPOSED TO WORK

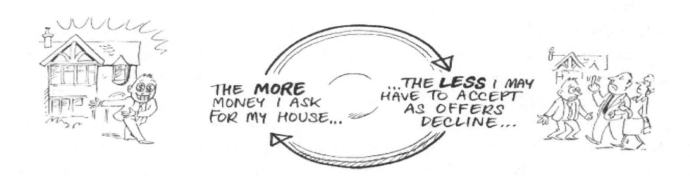

But there are exceptions...

FAST RISING PRICES ATTRACT SPECULATORS

Markets are supposed to be in equilibrium as in the top picture. The more I ask from my house the fewer come forward to buy it, but if I lower the price I will attract more buyers. The demand and supply curves will cross in the middle of the graph. So far so good, but it all depends on the motivation of my buyer. Suppose he is buying my house not to live in, but to sell on to someone else. He stops asking whether this is worth it to him but asks instead, "will someone buy it from me for even more money a year from now?" In a market where house prices are rising 10% a year, a $500,000 purchase will net him $50,000 capital gain. But note this rate of price increase cannot be long sustained. The bubble will burst. Moreover, the buyer is no longer making his own decision but speculating on what others will decide, which is an extremely hazardous guess. John Maynard Keynes likened this to a beauty pageant where you had to choose the contestant others would vote for. Note that while negative feedback can be postponed, it will return and the crash will be so much larger for its length of absence. When this happens, you may lose the game of musical chairs and a zero-sum game has winners gaining at the expense of losers with no wealth actually created.

Adam Smith's dictum is reversible

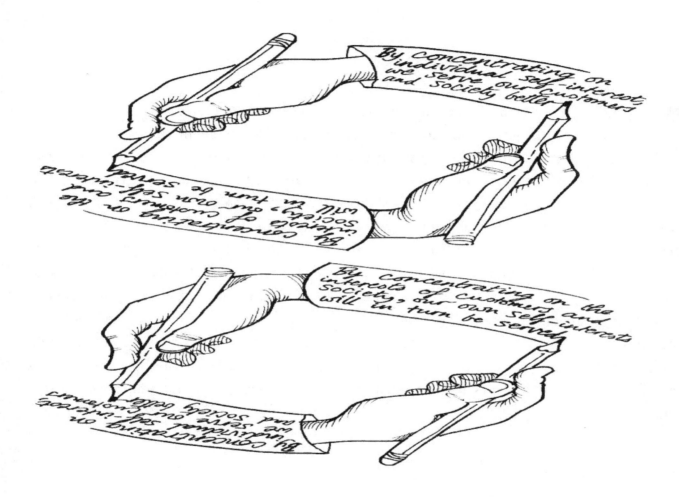

Self-interest triggers service to the customer, and vice versa. Smith was half-right.

Adam Smith's invisible Hand is in fact two hands, both visible. You can gain from consciously pursuing your own self-interest and profitability as in the upper diagram. This can lead to customers being better served and the public interest benefitting, possibly, but not necessarily, by accident. You can also gain by consciously pursuing the kind of baked goods customers said they liked and purchased in greater quantities, thereby possibly, but not necessarily, serving your own self-interest. Note the ambiguity in the pictures opposite. Which of the two hands is drawing and which is being drawn? By far the most favourable result is achieved by mobilizing both egoism and altruism and having these serve each other. The more I care that customers liked the bread I baked, the better position I am in to give them more of what they most enjoyed. The keener I am to profit and serve my own ends, the harder I will work to satisfy customers. Each value pushes the other into greater expression. Who does not want to be respected in his/her own town or village? Our lives amount to what we have done for others. We ourselves will be gone. However, self-interest is with us from infancy onwards. It takes a life-time of learning to truly appreciate others. Here lies the missing ingredient in business today. To quote Robbie Burns, "Can we come to see others as others see us?" Therein lies the art of living and if that is profitable, we can afford to do still more.

THE CHINESE HAVE GRASPED THE CIRCULAR NATURE OF WEALTH CREATION

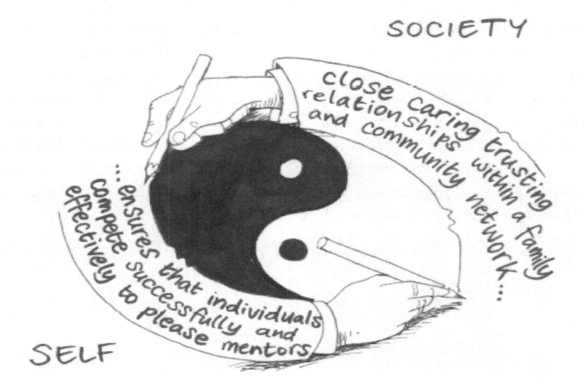

TWO VISIBLE HANDS:
THE CONFUCIAN ETHIC

SOCIETY

close caring trusting relationships within a family and community network...

...ensures that individuals compete successfully and effectively to please mentors

SELF

WHICH SYSTEM COMPETES BETTER IS A NO-BRAINER.

One simple reason the Chinese are growing at three to five times the rate of most Western countries is the way they think, which is far better attuned to our post-capitalist era. Yin-Yang is very much an ancient folk wisdom, a circle of eternal return which shifts back and forth in harmony. A major Chinese business value is guanxi, which refers to how well people relate and understand each other's needs. Relationships often start with a gift but it is vital that the need of the recipient is well-read. Within 24 hours of visiting a Chinese host with a battered suitcase, one of the authors had received a new one from that host! But the author thereby incurred an obligation to reciprocate. He now had to study his host carefully and ask himself what the host lacked. Favours and kindnesses tend to escalate on both sides which will deepen the relationship. The giver may be out of pocket unless the favour is returned. If you wish the relationship to be equal, you must give back as good as you get. There are guanxi networks in which the failure to reciprocate or to help when asked can lead the ingrate to lose face before other members. Relationships are often deep and long-term. One source of guanxi is the weaker rule of law in China and the need to settle disputes privately and justly. A mutual friend may be called upon and many arbitrations are win-win. Guanxi can also apply to the values sought by the parties so that close caring relationships in the picture opposite are seen as in the self-interests of both parties. The ethics of guanxi are Confucian and have to do with the duty to meet obligations. They are also associated with gangqing or empathy for another person. Relationships between native Chinese and the diaspora are known as the "bamboo network" and are responsible for the vigorous growth of the home country assisted by Chinese networks across the world.

d) AT THE HEART OF NATURE IS PARADOX: TWO WAYS OF KNOWING

PARTICLES

WAVES

LEFT BRAIN

RIGHT BRAIN

SCIENCE IS THE INTERACTION OF OUR NERVOUS SYSTEMS WITH WHATEVER IS OUT THERE.

What do we mean that science is paradoxical? Science is not the "way things really are." Science is an interaction between human sense impressions, plus instruments and the wider universe we inhabit. Science is the response of the human nervous system to what we encounter. If we use certain instruments like a "particle-detector" then we will discover a physical world full of particles. If on the other hand we use a wave-detector then, lo and behold, we will discover a world full of waves. We have helped to construct what it is we encounter. What we discover depends on the instruments we have used and our choice of instruments. A paradigm is a set of assumptions we make before we start looking. If we are looking for facts, units, objects and data we will start counting bits and pieces. If we are looking for waves, currents, patterns, systems and wholes we will start scanning. The left hemisphere of the human brain conceives of objects, words, units and numbers. The right hemisphere of the human brain conceives of movement, music, spaces and designs relations. A bundle of nerves called the corpus callosum joins the two. Since we have two distinct ways of conceiving the world, we understand the wider world in two different ways. Hence paradox is at the heart of science. Niels Bohr, the famous physicist, has the Yin-Yang symbol in his family coat-of-arms. He proposed the Principle of Complementarity that physics consists of waves and particles, but we cannot see these at the same moment. We must first select our instrument. Werner Heisenberg spoke of the Uncertainty Principle. We can locate the position of a particle, but will then lose sight of its momentum. We can estimate its momentum only to lose sight of its position.

Objects and Waves: Feng Shui and Chinese folk wisdom

Rocks and ripples: two approaches to reality.

Feng Shui is a Chinese metaphysical system used to arrange objects in an aesthetic and effective way so that energy runs through them and the occupants can tap into this energy. It is much used in the design of living spaces, in architecture, landscaping and restaurants where it is used to create ambience. It is akin to Chinese medicine in as far as its practices are handed down the generations. It has multiple connections to Taoism and to Yin-Yang thinking and interprets the animals in the Chinese calendar. It is not "scientific" in the sense of surviving scepticism and doubt in laboratory settings. It is generally given little credence outside China and Chinese communities in other lands. We raise it because it reflects Chinese culture and Chinese folk wisdom. The image opposite shows the importance of balance, harmony and aesthetics. What is valuable is visually elegant and forms a pattern. Note also that it includes both realms of science, science as objects and atoms and science as ripples, waves and frequencies. It is not clear in the image opposite where the ripples originate – perhaps from the stone being set down, but other versions depict water flowing through a hollow stick of bamboo and rippling the surface. The Chinese think very inclusively and do not regard rocks and whirlpools as twin perils as much as a coherent vision of reality. These are two equally valid ways of looking at the world and understanding it.

᪐

Water Logic 1: waves operating in the frequency realm

Concern with Profit

Concern with the growth of people and a sustainable planet

Interference waves can create aesthetic patterns (top right), severe conflict (centre), or total contradiction and confusion (bottom left).

Are we perhaps operating with the wrong logic, at least in regard to business and socio-political affairs? We assume business operations to be like 19th century physics, with numerous hard objects that bang into each other in sequences of cause and effect. We assume that some "independent variable" must be in control of some "dependent variable" so we can predict precisely what someone will do. We will scientifically make people work harder by controlling them! This is a ludicrous proposition and if remotely possible, an attack on democracy and a denial of freedom. Yet there is a whole different realm of science, that is unlike Newtonian physics and which the social sciences have largely ignored. We refer to the frequency realm, the world of brain-waves, water-waves, sound waves and music, electro-magnetic waves, light-waves, micro-waves, waves of gravity, x-rays, gamma-rays, ultra-violet rays, Kondratiev waves in economics, socio-linguistic waves, radio-waves and so on. If our brains produce waves would this not permeate everything? It was Edward de Bono who suggested we use "water logic". Waves interfere with each other like ripples on a pond crossing each other to produce waves-within-waves, some of great beauty. Waves in music harmonize or clash in discord. They moderate, influence, nudge and permeate each other with sensibility. Opposite we have considered two seemingly opposed values. Concern with Profit is on the vertical axis, Concern with People and Planet on the lateral axis. If these are hard objects like billiard balls, they will collide, but if they are wave forms they can be fine-tuned. Suppose they are wave forms then three possibilities arise. They form a contradiction and so cause logic and business to fail, see bottom left. They are mutually hostile and each must fight to win (see the centre of the picture). Finally, they are potentially harmonious, elegant, fitting, aligned and synergistic and customers, governments and employees will support this great movement to save us all. There are millions of green jobs to be created among waste-reducing employees using renewable, free energy. Were we to work with rather than against Nature just imagine how great our empowerment!

WATER LOGIC 2: SOCIAL ENTERPRISE AS INTERFERENCE WAVES

SOCIAL ENTERPRISE CAN PLOUGH ALL ITS PROFITS BACK INTO EXPANSION AND STAND UP TO GREED.

We earlier argued that value creation more nearly resembled waves with frequency and amplitude, than they did rocks of righteousness or flint-like integrity. When waves interact, they form interference patterns illustrated opposite, similar to dropping pebbles into a pond and watching the ripples cross. These patterns are often highly aesthetic. In music made by sound-waves there can be wonderful harmonies, waves-within-waves, with variations on a beat-frequencies, or descants in a hymn sung by a choir. The Deity is said to be Lord of the Dance and religions try to bind us with music. Ever present in music is point and counterpoint and the variations between. These are elegant and a delight to the ear. Opposite we have asked why For-profit organizations might not "interfere" with Non-profit organizations and their purposes to form Social Enterprises, which both serve people and renew themselves by ploughing profits back into their efforts. Might consumers choose to buy not just the product but the character of the supplying organization? The world-wide success of The Body Shop, Interface Carpets, Desso, and Ben and Jerry's show that such appeals work well and customers are capable of thinking of more than just themselves. Moreover, enterprises whose appeal attracts customers can grow larger and larger while government supplied welfare hangs by a thread in many countries and must typically be slashed when the International Monetary Fund comes to a nation's aid. The problem with Non-profit is its small scale; it needs to beg and only those with money can afford to be noble and rise above their fellows. The problem with For-profit enterprise is that all too easily it becomes an end itself. We need hybrids made of both. Few people can afford altruism for long. They can help others in the process of helping themselves. Big profitable companies can pay non-profits to assess their levels of social responsibility and provide early detection when things go wrong. In turn, the Non-profits could testify that progress had been made and goals had been fairly met and could certify this to customers.

e) Nature is fractal and largely paradoxical

Here is a skeleton of a hydrangea leaf

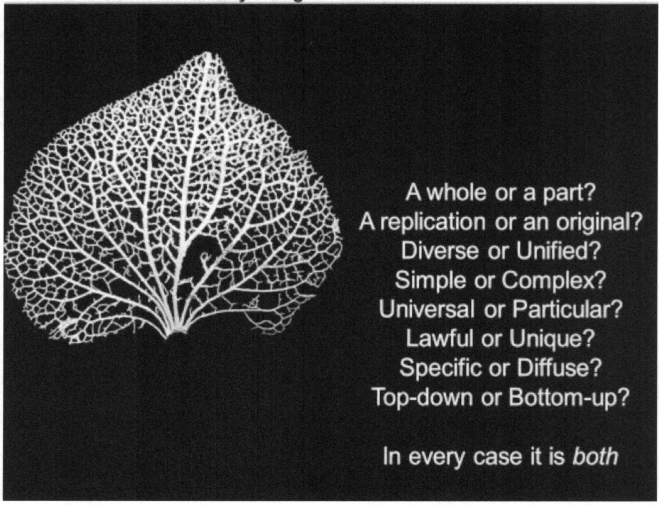

A whole or a part?
A replication or an original?
Diverse or Unified?
Simple or Complex?
Universal or Particular?
Lawful or Unique?
Specific or Diffuse?
Top-down or Bottom-up?

In every case it is *both*

THE ESSENTIAL AMBIGUITY OF NATURAL FORMS.

The word fractal means "the same from far as from near". It is similar to its parts in some way and is infinitely so, rather like a cauliflower. Large parts of nature are fractals. Look at a tree and it has a distinctive shape with branches diverging from a trunk, twigs diverging from branches, leaves diverging from twigs. If you look carefully at the leaf you will see a tiny tree in its structure, with spines that mimic the larger tree of which it is a part. Opposite is the dried skeleton of a hydrangea leaf. It is a whole or a part? Certainly, it is the part of a larger plant but it is also a whole in its own right with parts of its own. Is it a replication by a computer or a leaf grown naturally? It could be either. An algorithm can be used to create a fractal, but you can pick one in your garden. Is it simple or complex? Take a choice. Does the base serve the top or the top serve the base? Is it lawful or unique? Laws of life produce unique configurations. You will not find another leaf quite like it. Is it an object or a pattern, a microcosm or a macrocosm? Does it diverge or converge? It diverges bottom to top but converges top to bottom. The natural world makes nonsense of our polarizations of our either-or debates. If we want to grow our economies we must learn to reconcile values in ways similar to life-forms, to differentiate yet integrate, centralize what is decentralized in patterns of evolving symmetry.

FRACTALS IN THE NATURAL WORLD

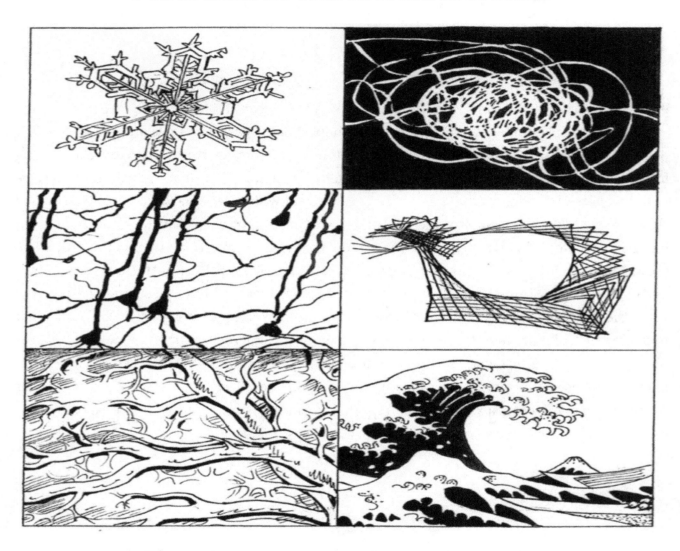

FRACTAL FORMS ARE IN ART AND IN NATURAL PHENOMENA.

The pictures opposite are all fractals occurring in nature and all are paradoxical in their evolving symmetries. A fractal has been defined as an abstract process used to simulate naturally occurring processes. Frost on a window pane is fractal as is forked lightening in the sky. Fractals are infinitely self-similar, yet different in scale. Top-left is a snowflake. It starts a seed crystal and as it falls through bands of colder and warmer air adds ice crystals to which ever arm is shorter which produces its imperfect symmetry. No two snowflakes are alike yet all have similar structures. Top right are the brain-waves on a recording machine of a woman solving a mathematical puzzle. Middle left are the dendrites in the human brain that make connections between distinct pieces of information, sharply defined yet meaningfully joined. Middle right is the computer print-out of a beating heart. The healthy heart beats faster or slower according to challenges faced. Bottom left is the blood circulation system in the human body with veins and arteries. And bottom right is the famous Japanese wood-cut by Hokusai entitled 'The Great Wave'. This is fractal because the foam at the crest of each wave mimics the design of the whole picture.

IS THE HUMAN CONDITION JANUS-FACED?

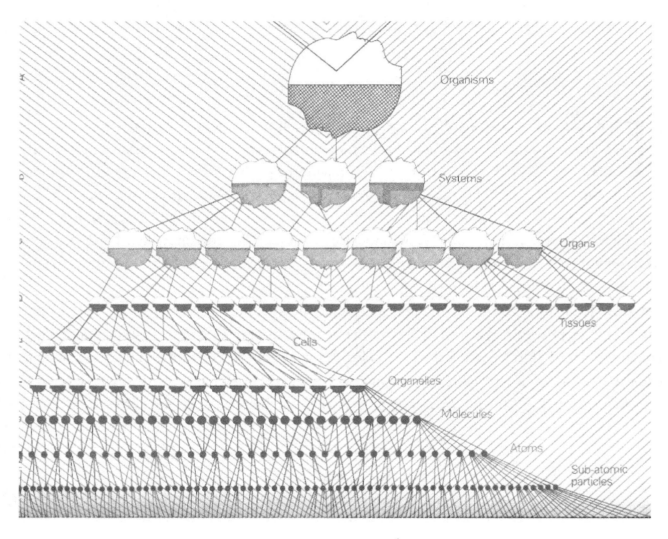

Organisms

Systems

Organs

Tissues

Cells

Organelles

Molecules

Atoms

Sub-atomic particles

JANUS, THE ROMAN GOD OF ARRIVAL AND DEPARTURE.

The late Arthur Koestler used the Roman god of Arrival and Departure, Janus, to explain our biology. The effigy stood before the front door of many Roman houses and blessed those who came in and went out. It faced outwards and it faced inwards and looked in both directions. He coined the word "holarchy" to express what he meant. A holarchy is a part to elements above it and a whole to the elements beneath it. Hence the human organism is a whole to the nervous systems beneath, which are parts to the organism above it. Our parts have considerable autonomy. One drives a car thinking of our next appointment, not of changing gear or applying the brake, as these have become habitual sub-systems. Our private parts rise to the occasion, or not! The quick-sketch artist leaves it to her hand. Koestler was pessimistic about the survival of the human race. This was because we got our parts and wholes badly mixed up. We seemed unable to manage dilemmas like autonomy vs dependence, aggression vs intimacy, competition vs cooperation. We constantly failed to understand that cooperation among the parts could fuel the fierce competition in the whole and that excess at one level could lead to excess at higher or lower levels. If we look at Koestler's book titles we can appreciate how he thought, *Arrival and Departure, Darkness at Noon, The Yogi and the Commissar, Insight and Outlook, The Lotus and the Robot, Dialogue and Death, The Challenge of Chance* and of course *Janus.* Condemned to death in the Spanish civil war, he had encountered his own end. He looked into the crucibles that others avoided. The branching out of the holarchy is more extensive than shown opposite. The organism is the member of a group and the group makes up the nation. Many pathologies arise from over/under-identification of the self with society. We are alive knowing we will die and this haunts us, "better a terrible end than endless terror." Paradox was essential to how Koestler thought and to his classic *The Act of Creation* which described highly improbable yet meaningful connections.

F) HOW WE THINK IS AN ATTEMPT TO IMPOSE ORDER:
1. NORMA, THE 'AVERAGE WOMAN'

HOW AVERAGE KILLS DIVERSITY.

Social science is faced with turmoil, argues Todd Rose of the Harvard School of Education. People do the most extraordinary things and take on a wide variety of appearances. How can we bring order to this sea of chaos? How can you create a science out of such infinite variety? How can people who leap all over the stage be replaced by hard facts that stand still long enough to be counted? In 1926, the Cleveland Board of Education invented the idea of Norma, the normal, average woman. They even had her sculpted from measurements supplied by 15,000 women. For some reason she became seen as an ideal woman, an embodiment of her gender, and was featured in *Time* as representing the American Look. Suddenly women wanted to look like Norma and came forward to be compared with her. But here the disappointment began; only 40 of the 3,864 women who presented themselves looked even remotely like Norma. The rest were abnormal! There were similar problems for the US Airforce seeking out the average pilot so the average cockpit could be designed around him. Once designed, most pilots remained seriously uncomfortable and performed poorly in environments unsuited to them.

We can see opposite that the average woman (or pilot) does not exist. She is a mental construct we have imposed upon our data in an attempt to impose sameness on variety and discipline upon recalcitrant humanity. Moreover, the variety of forms womanhood can take is far more interesting, colourful and impressive than Norma. We can see opposite that untypical woman is by far the more diverting and interesting; in fact, the more improbable the better! A female judge is all the more fascinating for being scarce. She must really have distinguished herself to get where she is. The Tyranny of the Average must be overthrown. Rose puts forward three principles; that of jaggedness, that of context and that of pathways. We have to value the uneven, jagged natures of human beings. We have to create a context for the individual person (e.g. moveable seats for pilots and retractable joy-sticks). We have to design a pathway to learning that respects uneven talents and anchors the student in what she or he excels at. You learn what your greatest talent and passion needs for its success. You do not compare yourself invidiously to some standard but grow around your strength.

How we think imposes order: 2. The blind men & the elephant

Though each was partly in the right, there were all in the wrong.

In our desperation to find order amid chaos, we impose part-truths on the complexity of life. The legend of the six blind men of India investigating the elephant is well known. It is a warning against all superficial and partial ways of seeing reality or, in the context of this book, our socio-political economy. Each "wise" man feels another part of the creature and insists (going clockwise) that it is "really" a spear, a fan, a wall, a tree, a rope and a snake. Each insists he is right and others are wrong. Each man clings to his abstract reductionism.

And so these men of Hindustan/ Each argued loud and long Though each was partly in the right/ They all were in the wrong

Relationships to other people are complex and there is always more to discover, always another point of view, always something we have missed. The great enemy is not ignorance but part-truth. Are we self-interested, for ever competing, and serpentine in our calculations? The answer is yes but there is another side to all these observations, a fuller reality. The reason we need justice, fairness, dialogue, democracy and conversation is that these are the only way the missing information can reach us. The view from the bottom needs to qualify the view from the top or the nation sickens. Markets may be a collection of things but life is a pattern which connects. If we fail to see this pattern we are seriously incomplete not just in knowledge but in ourselves. Among other goals, this book is a search for the whole, for larger and wider meanings, higher goals to which to dedicate our lives.

∽

HOW WE THINK IMPOSES ORDER:
3. ABSTRACTIONS AS SHADOWS

THE SHADOWS OF PLATO'S CAVE WERE NOT ENOUGH.

One problem with abstracting from reality is that we only capture part of it. Classical economics assumes that we all pursue our rational self-interest and any evidence contrary to this does not get modelled or abstracted. Much of what we regard as human and humane is simply ignored as irrational - quite a put-down! The images opposite show two rival models or abstractions. Are the phenomena we are investigating rectangular (top left) or are they shaped like an ellipse (bottom right)? It is often thought that science tests such things. It does test propositions within its paradigm (pattern of thought) but not that pattern itself. Indeed, science progresses from funeral to funeral, since very few of us put our underlying assumptions to the test. There are societies for the Advancement of Rectangles and Societies for the Advancement of Elliptical views. Very few of their adherents change their views in their life-times. It is only because we die that understanding can move on and new conceptions arise.

What the figure opposite shows is that models and abstractions are like shadows cast on walls. If you shine a light on one side of a cylinder you will indeed get a rectangle. The abstraction is not so much wrong as incomplete. If on the other hand you shine a light from the top of the cylinder you will see an ellipse. This is also incomplete rather than wrong. It is only if we combine these two ways of thinking that we get the truth, which is more multi-dimensional and complex than either of our two models. This is why relationships among equals are so important to any advance in the human condition, including the capacity to create wealth and grow our economy. Classical economics is not wrong but seriously incomplete. Keynesianism is not wrong but incomplete. We have to search for the place where they can relate effectively and complete one another. We have to encourage dialogue between part truths. The efficient market hypothesis is not without some truth. Markets do self-correct some of the time, but there are so many exceptions that we need a far more complex calculation to know when to intervene or when to leave well alone. Understanding the larger whole depends on relationships, not just between people but between ideas. Volume 2 will give many concrete examples.

How stories we tell reveal the culture of a company

REPEATED NARRATIVES REVEAL WHAT IS RIGHT OR WRONG ABOUT A CULTURE, WITH WARNINGS AND APPRECIATIONS.

Opposite are four corporate stories. The less entertaining of these are often the most important, as they issue warnings or express appreciations. At top left, Refinery Fire tells of a personal assistant to the head of Shell in Australia. His boss looked out of the window to see the refinery twenty miles down the coast was on fire. He urgently dispatched his assistant to report. But the car pool refused to let him drive a vehicle that did not express his correct seniority! The story points to rules overcoming discretion and common sense. Revson's Revenge at bottom right is just the opposite. Here Charles Revson of Revlon demanded that those passing through Reception sign against their time of arrival and put the new receptionist in charge. When he picked up the book she repeated that she had been told that the book was not to be removed from Reception. He said "When you pick up your last pay check this evening, ask them who I am." This story says "personal power is more important than rules." In the centre of the picture is the reason copywriters were not allowed to speak to clients at an advertising agency at which CMH-T once worked. An important client got stuck in an elevator and a passing copywriter on the landing said "Never mind, we'll feed you through the bars." Finally, IBM had a young 90 lb female security guard, the wife of a soldier fighting in Vietnam, at the gate of their Defence Division. She refused admittance to the CEO, Jim Watson, because he was not wearing his security badge. He laughed and said "She's right. We make the rules, we keep them." He returned to his office to retrieve the badge. The story celebrates the reconciliation of Rules with Particular Discretion and with exceptions. It says "Those making the rules will support your discretion in applying them, even when personally involved." This otherwise unremarkable story was re-told thousands of times in IBM because it meant something.

SEE THAT THINGS ARE HOPELESS YET BE DETERMINED TO MAKE THEM OTHERWISE

determined to make them otherwise

See that things are hopeless yet...

COMETH THE HOUR, COMETH THE MAN OR WOMAN WITH JUST THE RIGHT VALUES' COMBINATION

Winston Churchill may seem an odd choice for this book and in many respects like women's rights, the future of the empire and economic policy, he was behind the times. But nations and whole civilizations face crises from time to time, which only a particular combination of values can avert. 'Cometh the hour...cometh the right values' combination will do. Churchill lived up to the axiom coined by Scott Fitzgerald. "The test of a first-rate intelligence is to hold two opposed ideas in your mind at the same time and still retain your capacity to function. You must, for example, be able to see that things are hopeless, yet be determined to make them otherwise." No one was so pessimistic about Hitler, and rightly so, than Churchill was. He could not have mistaken the odds stacked against Britain, yet his determination to make it otherwise was tenacious, and the tension between these values did not break apart. When victory came he was no longer the man of the moment. In volume II of this book we will see that such tenacity may again be needed, a conservatism that does not yield to populist rage – not without fascist themes- and upholds democracy, a radicalism that creates new and better systems of authority. Capitalism has created vast wealth but we desperately need to broaden public access to this and be fair to all. We cannot become so hopeless that our determination snaps.

HOW BREXIT CUTS US INTO QUARTERS

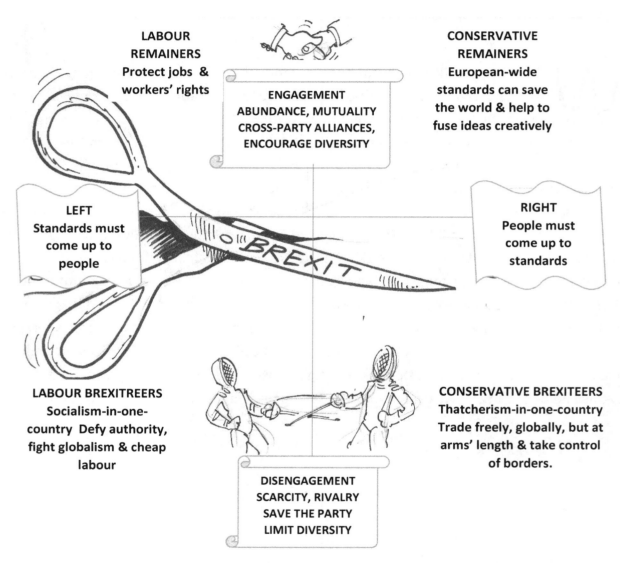

LABOUR REMAINERS
Protect jobs & workers' rights

ENGAGEMENT
ABUNDANCE, MUTUALITY
CROSS-PARTY ALLIANCES,
ENCOURAGE DIVERSITY

CONSERVATIVE REMAINERS
European-wide standards can save the world & help to fuse ideas creatively

LEFT
Standards must come up to people

RIGHT
People must come up to standards

LABOUR BREXITREERS
Socialism-in-one-country Defy authority, fight globalism & cheap labour

DISENGAGEMENT
SCARCITY, RIVALRY
SAVE THE PARTY
LIMIT DIVERSITY

CONSERVATIVE BREXITEERS
Thatcherism-in-one-country
Trade freely, globally, but at arms' length & take control of borders.

NO MAJORITY FOR ANY ONE QUADRANT

The British Parliament has been paralysed since the Brexit vote of 2016. It has rejected Mrs. May's deal but there is barely a majority of any other plan of action. Why is this? It is because Brexit opens up a new divide that like our pair of scissors opposite cuts through both parties so that we now have four quadrants, none of which commands a majority. We will try to explain this without damning anyone, ridiculing anyone, or faulting their logic. Indeed, they are all quite logical. The problem lies in different cultural premises and basic assumptions which often lie there unexamined. Remainers at the top of the diagram want to ENGAGE with Europe, Leavers at the bottom want to DISENGAGE. Remainers want the kind of freedom partners allow each other within relationships. Leavers believe that such relationships weaken freedom to act and go one's own way. Remainers see a world of ABUNDANCE where mental constructs can be turned into real products and services. There is enough for everyone. Leavers see a world of economic SCARCITY. There is never enough to go around and London, the City and the privately educated are getting the most of what there is. Remainers see a world of MUTUALITY, see the handshake at the top, in which the UK and the other 27 strengthen one another. Leavers see a world of RIVALRY, albeit non-violent, where the most competent attract the most money and manage it better than others could, see the fencing match at the bottom. Parliament is actually closer to a fencing match with colourful words and wit as foils in an everlasting adversary game, where one side wins and the other loses. Cutting words are more memorable. The Remainers see cross-party, cross-country alliances. Leavers want to save Socialism and the Conservative party, at almost any cost.

Labour Brexiteers (lower left quadrant) want Socialism-in-one-country and to defy authority and self-styled experts. Conservative Brexiteers (lower right quadrant) want Thatcherism-in-one-country and to trade freely with the whole world but at arm's length and sword's length – like fencers. Labour Remainers (top left quadrant) want to protect workers jobs and rights, while Conservative Remainers (top right quadrant) want to create wealth from the creative fusion of diverse values. Because Leavers are fencers, they claim that Europe-will-blink-first, keep "no deal" on the table so they panic and give way, that Europe always yields at the last moment and that parliamentarians should be forced to vote for May by worse alternatives, restricted choices & deadlines. Because leavers are hand-shakers they believe both sides can win and Europe wishes us well. All this cuts across traditional left/right dichotomies, where the left extols people and doubts standards, while the right extols standards and doubts people. Is diversity a threat as leavers believe or an opportunity to be more innovative as Remainers believe? Is the Free Market all the authority we need or must Europe help us save the environment and tame the Internet? For Remainers, members of Parliament represent constituents rather than obey them as would delegates and as persons-of-conscience they must uphold the nation. For Leavers the "people have spoken" and the Commons must enact the will that people expressed, or stand accused of betrayal. The manifestos of both parties promised to enact Brexit-of-a-kind, but what kind?

"I HAVE A DREAM..."

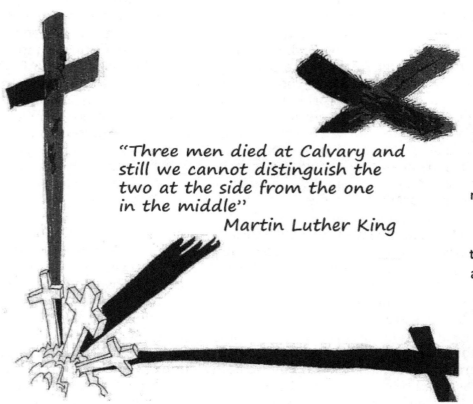

"Three men died at Calvary and still we cannot distinguish the two at the side from the one in the middle"
Martin Luther King

"There is some talk about what might happen to me from some of our sick white brothers, but that does not matter to me now, because I've been to the mountain top and I've *seen* the Promised Land. I may not get there with you but we as a people *will* get to the Promised Land. Mine eyes have seen the glory of the coming of the Lord." Speech the night before his murder.

THOSE WHO KNOW NOT WHAT THEY WOULD DIE FOR, HAVE NOT YET LIVED

The cross in the middle is akin to the psychic crucifixion we endure when we reconcile values. Martin Luther King was brilliant at weaving together values; soul and power became soul power, putting your body on the line to be kicked and beaten integrating Mind and Body and teaching your body not to panic in the face of oppression. Suffering is redemptive, he taught. He marched as in war before kneeling as in prayer and he defied the law while accepting its penalties. He asserted himself but non-violently. He cited ancient scripture while seeking future freedom. He likened a despised minority of Americans to the Chosen People of God marching to the land promised by America's constitution. He broke Jim Crow laws but did so in a manner and with such courtesy that new laws could and were fashioned out of this. He demonstrated publicly that whites and blacks could march together, pray together, work together in harmony. The bonds created by common danger were unbreakable. He had ideals he turned into realities. He married passion with an iron discipline of not striking back. He dissented against how the USA treated black people but remained loyal to its constitution. He bought the Other World to the politics of This World and religious sentiment to the secular. The middle cross in the picture opposite is neither of the two extremes which tear us apart, nor is it compromise, trade-off or "miscegenation". It is a plea that in a world of polarities we integrate not simply black and white, but opposed values in general. He was a humble servant to his cause, but that cause raised him to the pinnacle of fame. He was a Servant Leader par excellence. Christ was crucified between two thieves. Each thought of himself and not of victims. Each preyed on his fellow man. Yet there was redemption for at least one of them, from the man who stood between fanaticisms with arms extended, reaching outwards to our common humanity. We must unite the secular and the sacred.

BRITISH CAPITALISM BEGAN WITH A VERITABLE RENAISSANCE MAN

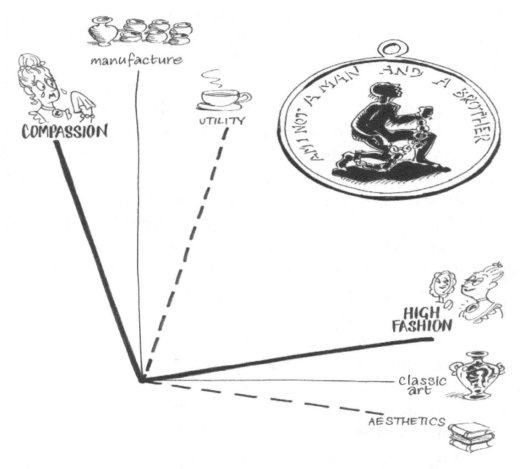

JOSIAH WEDGWOOD, A CONTEMPORARY OF ADAM SMITH, WAS A VISIBLE REFUTATION OF HIS THESIS OF NARROW SELF-INTEREST

Josiah Wedgwood, the 18th-century English entrepreneur, was the wealthiest innovator of his age and a contemporary of Adam Smith. Strangely the latter was not influenced by his example at all, despite the fact that he was de facto leader of the merchant class Smith described. Wedgwood was a world citizen and hugely influenced by Chinese porcelain and its classical motifs and showed that manufacturing china could be a fine art. He married classic art with modern manufacturing and everyday utility with aesthetics. He used classical images in his Jasperware from Ancient Greece and Rome, which were being unearthed at that time to wide admiration. He was a Unitarian believing in the unity of all sects of Christianity and subscribed to a new church which would reconcile science with religion. He himself was elected to the Royal Society for his success in measuring the temperature in kilns. He risked censure in supporting the American side in the War of Independence and had an extensive correspondence with William Wilberforce about the abolition of slavery, a cause in which his sister was a major mover. He showed that Compassion and High Fashion could be combined by dint of his famous medallion of a kneeling slave, inscribed with the words. "Am I not a man and a brother?" Large versions of this were hung on walls, with smaller versions as brooches worn by women and even hat-pins. He showed it to Benjamin Franklin who had it imported to America where it did a roaring export trade. He was not only a businessman but a leading scientist and intellectual in touch with most of the luminaries of his age.

He built model villages for his workers, had them all trained as craftsmen and inoculated against small-pox from which he had suffered in his youth. He introduced the first illustrated catalogue and the first money-back guarantee for china shattered by rough roads. His was the first travelling sales force. He financed canals to float his produce to markets. He gave his china free to all the crown-heads of Europe, knowing that when they used it guests would want to buy. He persuaded Queen Charlotte to endorse Queen's Ware and invented the notion of branding. The money he left his daughter ended up sponsoring the Charles Darwin and *The Origin of Species.* He was the greatest entrepreneur of his century. Is this a vision of capitalism we have now lost but could regain?

VOLUME 2 OF THIS BOOK WILL ADDRESS REMEDIES: HERE IS A START

FUTURE AGES WILL WONDER AT US, AS THE PRESENT AGE WONDERS AT US NOW.

IF YOU ARE EVER FEELING DESPERATE, READ PERICLES' FUNERAL ORATION.

In Volume 2 we will look for inspiration to the Golden Age of Athens, the leadership of Pericles, soldier, aristocrat and orator, who decided to rule through democratic persuasion and the spoken word. This is the age that brought us theatre, democracy, the rule of law, medicine, poetry, history, sculpture, architecture, jury trials, competitive sports and humanism. Pericles gave his famous funeral oration for the first casualties returning from the war with Sparta, 80% of whose citizens were helots or slaves. With hindsight, it was the funeral of Athenian power, but it makes for a great summation of that city's place in world history. "Our constitution is called a democracy because power is in the hands not of a minority, but of the whole people. When it is a question of settling private disputes, everyone is equal before the law, when it is a question of putting one person before the other in positions of public responsibility, what counts is not membership of a particular class, but the actual ability of that person." The loss of young men in battle was as if "the nation had lost its spring time…They ran only from dishonour."

Pericles made a brilliant case for diversity as the path of mankind. "We throw our city open to the world and never let alien acts exclude the foreigner from any opportunity to observe us, although the eyes of the enemy may occasionally profit from our liberality…Because of the greatness of the city, the fruits of the whole earth flow in upon us, so that we enjoy the goods of other countries as freely as our own." He made an incisive definition of courage, which we will be following in volume II. "Many men are brave out of ignorance and when they think they begin to fear. We hold a man to be really brave who knows the sweetness of life, its joys and fragilities, and stills goes to face its perils." Volume 2 will ask why we work, why we create, why we seek meaning and to leave a legacy behind us, why industry and the creation of value comes before all else. Profit merely allows us to continue what we love. Pericles put it well, "Mighty are the monuments we have left…. future ages will wonder at us as the present age wonders at us now." Let us see if it is possible to rebuild this glory.

APPENDIX:
(NOTES ON PART 1)

1. IT IS STAKEHOLDERS WHO ARE DOING THE ACTUAL WORK

R. Edward Freeman puts the case well in his recent book *Stakeholder Theory: The State of the Art*, Cambridge University Press, 2010, although much of what he writes has long championed this view. Charles Handy has asked whether one person can be said to "own" another's creativity and productivity. Surely these are inalienable? *Waiting for the Mountain to Move*, Arrow Books, 1995 addresses this issue. The whole notion that those who do the real work are the mere "agents" of those who have purchased share certificates needs re-examination. A small minority of top managers have share-options which they can cash in at opportune moments. Lay-offs and redundancies will usually create a spike in the share-price, short-term of course.

2. RELATIONSHIPS AMONG STAKEHOLDERS ARE THE KEYS TO WEALTH CREATION

The whole idea of maximizing the self-interest of your unit can harm the other units in your industrial eco-system. A product cannot be the best if the suppliers providing the components are pushed into slashing costs and scrimping on quality. To exploit partners is to weaken yourself. Starve a small company of funds and it cannot grow to serve you better. What wins new orders is a combination of all those with a stake in the future of the company working with each other.

3. STAKEHOLDER CAPITALISM IS OVERTAKING SHAREHOLDER CAPITALISM

Stake holding is how all companies start. A founder or founders get an idea and ask enthusiasts for this idea to join them. They may work for next-to-nothing but share the proceeds. Rapid growth and many new jobs may be created at this stage, see Hermann Simon, *The Hidden Champions of the Twenty-First Century*, New York: Springer 2009. Germany's great strength is its three million Mittelstand, small or medium sized companies owned by families and thinking long-term about what grand-children will inherit. Very few of these become public companies, owned by shareholders, whose horizon is too often the next quarterly report. Catch-up, family-owned companies can "buy market share" by coming in with the cheapest offers. Public companies may then withdraw rather than squeeze their own profitability. The UK and the USA are both losing world market shares to those coming from behind.

4.   STAKEHOLDER CAPITALISM IS REPLACING SHAREHOLDER DOMINANCE

We believe that companies run by and for people with stakes in the outcome represent a superior model, see Will Hutton *How Good We Can Be,* London: Little Brown 2015

5.   B) SHAREHOLDER DOMINANCE: IS IT CANCEROUS?

Shareholders have every right to make profits on their investments. That is not the issue. The issue is whether they would make more profits by growing their employees, nurturing and helping their suppliers, delighting their customers, developing scientific knowledge and saving the environment. Josiah Wedgwood, Great Britain's first tycoon did all these things while fighting the slave trade, see Hilary Young *The Genius of Wedgwood* London: Victoria and Albert Museum, 1995. Besides *Conscious Capitalism* cited in the text see *Firms of Endearment* by Rajendra Sisodia, David B Wolfe, and Jagdish Sheth, Wharton School Publishing, 2007

6.   THE VICIOUS CIRCLE OF SHAREHOLDER DOMINANCE

What makes the situation worse is that there is no shortage of capital. There is a desperate shortage of skills and knowledge. Shareholder dominance exacerbates this injustice and reduces learning.

7. Disruptive innovation and hollowing out the corporation.

The film-clip of what Christensen told us is available from the publishers and may be viewed on-line. The idea that the firm is represented by its brand is a dangerous half-truth. Brands can be flimsy and ephemeral, especially when the real work behind them is being done in Singapore. A computer is not just a "good feeling", it operates and functions.

8. Is buying back your own shares a form of sterility?

For further insights into this process see *Fixing Global Finance* by Martin Wolf, Yale University Press, 2009

9. Why stakeholder companies are more likely to be raided

The discovery that companies who were the target of raiders were better managed than the average company was made by Geoff Mulgan in *The Locust and the Bee: Predators and Creators,* Princeton University Press, 2013. The locust gobbles up the busy fertilizing bee. See also Colin Mayer's *Firm Commitment: Why the corporation is failing us*, Oxford University Press, 2013. Cadbury's take-over by Kraft was an example.

10. Acquiring and taking over small companies rather than learning and growing oneself

The idea that a large company is better than a small company because it has more money and can buy it up, runs into the stubborn fact first pointed out in *In Search of Excellence* New York: Harper and Row 1982 by Thomas J Peters and Robert H Waterman Jr., that small companies are much more innovative by a factor of five or more. For more recent estimates see Will Hutton *How Good We Can Be* London: Little-Brown 2015

11. WALL STREET VS. MAINSTREET: IS FINANCE CONSTRICTING INDUSTRY?

The case that as Wall Street expands the rest of industry shrinks, has been made forcefully by Rana Foroohar one-time economics editor of *Time* and author of *Makers and Takers,* New York: Crown Business Books, 2016. She cites specifically Boris Cournede and Oliver Denk "Finance and Economic Growth in the OECD and G20 countries" Working Paper No. 1223, volume 1 New York: Elsevier, 2015 and Stephen G. Cecchetti and Enisse Kharroubi "Why does Financial Sector Growth Crowd Out Real Economic Growth?" Working Paper no.490 Bank of International Settlements 2015. See also "Reassessing the Impact of Financial Growth" Working Paper no 381, Bank of International Settlements, July 2012, by the same authors.

12. STAKEHOLDERS AND INDUSTRY ARE A MERE MEANS TO ENRICHING OWNERS

As we shall see later in this book, money is a great boon to creative persons and helps them a lot. But that is not to say that money induces people to be creative in the first place, quite the contrary. As Michael Porter has often pointed out, it is the seller of a business who makes money. Extracting money is the opposite from investing it. The Frisbee is a useful metaphor.

13. DO MONEY REWARDS KILL CREATIVE PROBLEM-SOLVING?

See Daniel H. Pink *Drive: The Surprising Truth About What Motivates Us* London: Canongate, 2009. See also his TED talk online and his talk to the RSA. The candle problem has a long research history with very consistent results acknowledged by the London School of Economics among others.

14. WHY PAY FOR PERFORMANCE FAILS AGAIN AND AGAIN

The best demolition of the stubborn habit of trying to pay for performance is by Alfie Kohn *Punished by Rewards,* Boston: Beacon Press, 2008. The picture comes from a similar thesis by Harry Levinson in *The Great Jackass Fallacy,* Harvard University Press, 1973.

15. WHY THE BONUS CULTURE IS TOO SIMPLISTIC TO WORK EFFECTIVELY

This is similar to Roger Fisher and his rule that you must be tough on the problem but tender on the person who has the problem, see *Getting to Yes* Harmondsworth, Penguin 1990. See also Edward G Lawler *High-Involvement Management,* San Francisco Jossey-Bass, 1986.

16. THE UK'S PAYMENT PROTECTION INSURANCE SCANDAL

This is well described by Will Hutton in *How Good We Can Be* Op. cit.

17. NO TWO COINS EVER CREATED A THIRD COIN OR EVER WILL

See Robert H Frank and Philip Cook, *The Winner-Take-All Society* London: Virgin 2010 and Gideon Rachman, *Zero-Sum World.* London: Atlantic Books, 2010. Lord Adair Turner startled his audience in his 2009 Mansion House speech by stating that finance was of limited social utility. He braced himself for angry rebuttals but there were few or none

18. WE HAVE TO BE MORE THAN BAR-CODES

Money and codes in general are abstractions. We need to ask ourselves what they leave out.

19. LEVERAGE AS THE GREAT TEMPTATION

Banks have been found to lend out thirty or more times the assets they hold. It is very rare for everyone to want their money back at the same moment, but this happens in crashes where panic spreads and it wipes out billions, see Martin Wolf *The Shifts and the Shocks* London: Allen Lane, 2013. See also John Lanchester, *Whoops: Why Everyone Owes Everyone and No One Can Pay,* Penguin Books, 2010

20. D) GROSS INEQUALITY: THE SOCIAL COST

In *The Balanced Scorecard* by Robert S Kaplan and David P Norton, Harvard Business Review Press, 1996, the authors state the importance of balancing the past financial performance of the company against its future learning goals. They make an excellent case for this, emphasising that finance looks to the past exclusively, see the Harvard Business Review January 1992. What they do not adequately warn us against is the colossal bias in favour of past financial results and the folly looking only backwards to the detriment of the future.

21. MONEY AND GROSS INEQUALITY: PANDORA'S BOX

The Spirit Level: Why Equality is Better for Everyone by Richard Wilkinson and Kate Pickett, is published by Penguin Books, 2010. We need to distinguish between values that describe end states, like how much money individuals are worth, and values describing processes, for example treating people as if they were our equals in order to learn more about them. Unequal earning encourages us to neglect the poor and give them no chance to influence us.

22. THE CONSEQUENCES OF WOMEN EARNING LESS

It is of interest that finance is the greatest offender in this regard. Does this monochrome world of more and less, fail to do justice?

23. THE FIERY TOMBSTONE OF OUR PREDATORY CAPITALISM

One more result of not listening to persons deemed unimportant. They died because they did not get a hearing from those who collected their rents and judged themselves infinitely superior.

24. ECONOMICS HAS LOST THE SOUL OF MANKIND

John Ruskin's famous essay "Unto This Last" is available in a collection of his works under this title edited by J D C Monfries, London University Tutorial Press, 1951

25. HOW IS CAPITALISM EVOLVING: TWO PROBLEMS AT LEAST.

The UK has now reached the point where obesity is more of a threat to life than malnutrition. Our consumer society weighs us down with debt and food. Cheap food is mostly junk food.

26. The Phenomenon of "Chi-merica"

Expressed in an internet essay by the two authors who treat it as a passing phenomenon, while we believe it is the result of national strategies.

27. The Fallacy of the more the better: Thinking in straight lines

Abraham Kaplan coined the phrase in *The Conduct of Inquiry* San Francisco: Chandler, 1964 and refers to taking something scientifically true in certain circumstances and generalizing it across the board.

28. The Dream of unbridled power and strength.

".... Gone to graveyards every one, When will they ever learn?" from the folk song 'Where Have All the Flowers Gone?' by Pete Seeger.

29. Should we all strive to be winners?

See John C Bogle Enough: *True Measures of Money, Business and Life.* John Wiley, 2009 and The Winner-Take-All Society op.cit.

30. Winning by carving off pieces of China

The West has forgotten the Opium Wars. China has not.

31 The Linear Harpoon and the Great White Whale

The moral is that life is circular and cause-and-effect thinking endangers life

32. Absolute values are palpably absurd. We should all laugh.

Explains why we start moralizing when planning to kill, like President Johnson praying over Vietnam.

33.　Thinking in straight lines 1: Abstract globalism

Of course, we are NOT saying that there is any moral equivalence between our efforts to globalize finance across the world and the murderous behaviour of the terrorists in attacking the World Trade Centre. We regard those who died as innocents. But we are drawing attention to the fact that attempts to universalize across the globe, triggers a very particular and very brutal backlash in those who feel excluded and are exceptions to our rules. Finance loses touch with humanity at its peril where that humanity erupts in a fury that assumes monstrous proportions. We need to face that reality, and leave room for those who think differently before they lose all sense of proportion and assail us.

34.　Thinking in straight lines 2: Quantity preferred to Quality

Also good on these subjects is *False Dawn: The Delusions of Global Capitalism* by John Gray, London: Granta, 2009

35.　Are we fighting people or serving them?

Strategy is a military metaphor and tends to stress fighting over serving, the straight line of the sword over the circle of the delivery and the payment for it.

36.　Top-down orders lead to blood, mud and futility

Henry Mintzberg is merciless on the subject of grand strategy by leaders. He likens it to God's creation with Henry in support of evolution as an alternative explanation. He shadowed several CEOs and found that so far from designing great plans of action, they were mostly fighting fires and reacting to events. Crafting Strategy, *Harvard Business Review*, March/April 1987 is a gem and argues that much of strategy emerges from the interface with customers and then bubbles up.

37. WHY LINEAR STRATEGIES FAIL. NO WORLD-BEATING STRATEGY IS POSSIBLE

For a comprehensive view of strategy see *The Strategy Process* by Henry Mintzberg and James B Quinn, New York: Prentice Hall, 1997. Alexander the Great lived in a day of near-zero information so armies did not know of his strategy in advance and were surprised and overwhelmed, but today we know what a company is doing quite easily and to do the same, leads to stalemate and mutual attrition. There is a need for originality.

38. STRAIGHT-LINE STRATEGIES LEAD US STRAIGHT INTO CONTRADICTION

Much of this is taken from *Strategic Synthesis* by Bob de Wit and Ron Meyer, Thompson Learning, 2005. However, there are more contradictions than syntheses and we have provided our own.

39. ALL VIABLE BUSINESS STRATEGIES ARE CIRCULAR, NOT STRAIGHT LINES.

If a strategy is to have successive moves, then you need to feedback the results.

40. THE RISE OF THE UNICORN

We are not advocates of the tactics of some Unicorn companies like Uber which has designed a superior technological system, but uses it to shake down those who drive for a living, see Trebor Scholz *Uberworked and Underpaid* Cambridge: Polity Press, 2017. It would be a simple matter to turn taxi-drivers into skilled guides to cities, specializing in different attractions. Yet the importance of Unicorns remains, because they have resisted shareholder power and recognized that it is averse to innovation and fast growth.

Notes on Part II

41. How the wealth-creating cycle works

To say that "shareholders come last" is NOT to say that they are least important. They are equals, but they do come last in time, insofar as what they collect has first to be created, see the MacArthur Foundation for the case that the economy is circular.

42. The circular process of wealth creation

This is what is referred to as the circular economy. It is not recycling alone which makes it circular but the mutual development of the stakeholders.

43. Segment 1: Employees are trained, skilled, educated, developed and kept well

No less an authority than Peter Drucker has long insisted that employees are knowledge workers, see *The Practice of Management,* New York: Harper and Row, 1954. Donald N. Michael has pointed out that we are all in a "learning race" see *Learning to Plan and Planning to Learn*, Miles River Press, 1997. Products are becoming more and more knowledge-intensive. It would pay nations to celebrate those companies that kept their workers well by monitoring their life-styles and intervening before they fell ill. It would help to give them meaningful goals to work for. What about a contest for the lowest health insurance claims? How much money does Johnson and Johnson save the NHS? Why not reward the company and publicise its efforts?

44. Segment 2: Suppliers are challenged, nurtured, developed and made prosperous.

Korean companies are famous for paying suppliers promptly, in some cases within three days in cash, see John Mackey and Raj Sisodia *Conscious Capitalism* Boston: Harvard Business School Press, 2013. Whole Foods takes great pride in the suppliers it has developed and will lend them money to help them over cash-flow crises.

45.   SEGMENT 3: HIGHER PRODUCTIVITY THAT DELIGHTS CUSTOMERS AND INCREASES REVENUE...

The list of beloved companies that treat their customers superlatively well has recently been updated, see *Firms of Endearment* op cit, and *Conscious Capitalism* op cit.

46.   SEGMENT 4 : THIS GROWS LOCAL COMMUNITIES AND SUSTAINS THE ENVIRONMENT...

It can of course be highly profitable to sustain and even improve the environment, see Amory and Hunter Lovins, and Paul Hawken in *Natural Capitalism* London: Little-Brown, 1999. The sun and wind are free and harnessing their energy lowers the cost year by year. High-tech companies increasingly rely on well-educated communities that surround them. It paid Motorola to sustain the Chicago public school system around them. The Apple 1 computer was given to every Californian high school at public expense.

47.   SEGMENT 5: WHILE PAYING TAXES TO GOVERNMENT WITHOUT RESISTANCE...

US companies vary considerably. Some like Johnson and Johnson pay corporate tax rates without resisting, others pay an effective tax of 5% or less but spend heavily on lawyers which constitute a "profit centre" for that company, albeit one that deprives the rest of us.

48.   SEGMENT 6: AND GIVING THE RESIDUE TO THE RAGING BULL WHO RE-INVESTS

The comparison between "firms of endearment" and stock price averages comes from *Conscious Capitalism* by Mackey and Sisodia op.cit. pp. 278-283

49.   HOW THE WEALTH-DESTRUCTION CYCLE WORKS

The irony is that we have known all this for years. In 1991, Harvard Business School Press published *Short-Term America* by Michael T. Jacobs. The financial system simply shrugs off inconvenient evidence of its short-comings, even as it sponsors members of Congress. Unless we first serve employees, suppliers and customers we cannot discover what the residue might have been, had we treated them properly.

50.   The Wealth-Destroying vicious Circle

The whole idea of ropes snapping and values coming part is from Gregory Bateson's description of schizmogenesis, "the growing split in the structure of ideas." See *Steps to an Ecology of Mind* New York: Ballantine, 1972 pp 61-72 The rope imagery is our own but conveys his meaning.

51.   Segment 1: More money for shareholders targeted before operations start...

For this development see R. Rajan and L. Zingales "Financial Dependence and Economic Growth" in *American Economic Review* 88 pp. 559-581, 1998. If you tell shareholders in advance what they are likely to receive then supplying this will be at the cost of other stakeholders who will be treated as a cost rather than an investment.

52   Segment 2 : And is wrested from staff via outsourcing and cost-cutting...

You do get lower labour costs via outsourcing but you lose face-to-face contact with the people working for you and manage by e-mail, rather than by sharing. Your foreign employees, seen as "low cost", are also being taught how to make your product and may one day challenge you with this knowledge. In the meantime, you have trashed all the local US suppliers that once worked for you, who may now be dispersed beyond recall. The Chinese are not plotting against US companies, they are simply falling in with their plans to enrich shareholders above all others.

53.   SEGMENT : SUPPLIERS HAVE PRICES CUT, SCRIMP ON QUALITY, ARE PAID LATE AND WILT....

Running suppliers against each other stops them from learning from their customers. If you have supplied a company for years you learn a lot about it and how to serve it more effectively. There is nothing wrong with telling your preferred supplier that he has to meet prices charged by competitors and give him time to do this. You can invest in your supplier and share the proceeds in the form of reduced prices. You can train his and your engineers together. You need his help to eliminate toxins from what is supplied, but failure to do this could sink you. How late companies pay their suppliers and the casualties therefrom should be published and considered when awarding contracts.

54. SEGMENT 4 : CUSTOMERS ARE OUTWITTED INTO BUYING BY CLEVER TACTICS...

See Al Gore on the sheer surfeit of our consumer society and the millions of hits by advertisers on each child. This is less wicked than wasteful, a much ado about nothing of importance and an invitation to over-indulgence, see *Our Choice: A plan to solve the climate crisis.* London: Bloomsbury 2009. Advertised products tend to be the most trivial and are aimed at low-commitment purchasers.

55.   SEGMENT 5 : SO THAT TRUST, COMMUNITY AND SUSTAINABILITY ALL SUFFER

For the costs involved in pollution, see *The Necessary Revolution:* London, Nicholas Brealey, 2008 by Peter Senge. Every bottle of cola requires fifty times its volume in fresh water and is worse for you than water, the absence of which could kill most of the earth's creatures.

56.   Segment 6: Profits are sent to tax-havens abroad, tax-avoidance pushed, and even....

For a wide-ranging commentary on all this folly see *Fools Gold; How Unrestrained Greed Corrupted a Dream* by Gillian Tett, London: Abacus, 2010

57.   The Bonds between shareholders and stakeholders are severed.

These and similar points are well made by Joseph E Stiglitz in *The Price of Inequality* London: Allen Lane 2012, and Paul Krugman *The Great Unravelling* New York: WW Norton, 2005. The needed wisdom is not absent but ignored. See also Robert Reich's online videos and his concern that "the band has snapped" and the USA is coming apart.

NOTES ON PART III

58.   THE SALIENCE OF WICKED PROBLEMS

A wicked problem is so called because it resists resolution and is deeply entangled within the system and attempts to deal with it alter many other elements, often for the worse. It is complex, pervasive, contradictory in appearance and keeps returning over the years to haunt once more, see *Wicked and Wise* by Alan Watkins and Ken Wilber London: Urbane Publications Ltd. 2015.

59   a) DIVERSITY VS ENGAGEMENT: OPPORTUNITIES AND DIRE THREATS

We are much indebted to Rollo May and his book *The Meaning of Anxiety,* New York: Norton, 1977. This may be the Achilles Heel of mankind. It seems human kind is totally unnerved by threats it cannot understand and because these are vague, free-floating and fill us with dread, we know not how to alleviate the feeling of being menaced. It is in this gloom of despair that unscrupulous leaders blame scapegoats. It is all the fault of Jews, immigrants, Mexicans, the Chinese, communists, Jesuits, witches, etc.

60   TURNING DIFFUSE ANXIETY INTO SPECIFIC FEARS

The driving force behind much persecution is to find some reason to cooperate. Since cooperation is the ethic of well-known scapegoats like Jews, Communists, Mexicans and the EU, only by believing that they are conspiring against us can we achieve the solidarity we crave. It is a case of America first, or taking back control of our boarders from ill-defined foes. Identity politics helps us define ourselves by what we are against; gays, Islam, abortion, uppity women etc.

61 SOME VALUE BIASES BEHIND BREXIT

Most of these arguments are taken from *Saving Britain: How we must change to prosper in Europe* Will Hutton and Andrew Adonis Abacus, 2018

62   b) Tension vs Relaxation: the roots of addiction to alcohol.

Gregory Bateson's famous essay "Towards a Theory of Alcoholism" is included in *Steps to an Ecology of Mind.* New York: Ballantine 1972. The reason alcoholism is a wicked problem that rarely goes away, is that self-manipulation is habitual; the more you use substances to relax or excite yourself, the less you will use another human being, so the lonelier and manipulative you become.

63   c)   Causation-Mutuality   Have we got the wrong paradigm?

The whole notion that social science is like 19th century physics and that we must predict and control the behaviour of our subjects as if they were dead objects is repellent. The subject of our studies should be human relationships to which we are one party and their aim should be enhanced mutuality between the persons concerned, the 'knower' and the 'known'. Simply interviewing someone has already started that mutuality and the aim is to bring the best out of that person.

64   Cause and effect hates mutuality and assails it

If you assume the right of your science to be independent while your subjects depend on your unilateral input, then you cannot and will not create a relationship and you kill mutuality.

65   Fortune Magazine used to celebrate America's 10 toughest bosses

The whole idea that your boss "causes" your behaviour and therefore deserves to earn multiples of your salary in ludicrous. The truth is that CEOs salaries are way up while performance is too often weakening. The best you get from shouting orders is sullen compliance, if not sabotage.

66   d) Right vs Left as stone statues on a deserted isle

"Rock of ages cleft to me, let me hide myself in thee." There is a persisting delusion that if we become rock-like in our certitude then we will survive. The truth is that only rocks will do so.

67   Left vs Right in politics as a wicked problem

The distinctions comes from Silvan Tomkins' essay, Left and Right: A basic dimension in ideology', in *The Study of Lives: Essays in Honour of Henry A Murray.* Robert White (ed) New York: Atherton, 1963. We have Einstein on the Left stating that the formulation of a problem is often more essential than its solution, while the logical positivists on the Right stating that science must be reduced to realities we can observe via objective agreement. What is immeasurable is unknowable.

68   e) Boom vs Bust: Are we addicted to boom and bust?

This is known as "cusp catastrophe" wherein the person or a whole group of persons tumble from one extreme to its opposite, see Denis Postle's *Catastrophe Theory* London: Fontana, 1980. For a more academic treatment try Christopher Zeeman *Catastrophe Theory: Selected Papers.* Reading: Benjamin 1977. Leaning too far left or right, towards boom or bust causes the middle ground to form a precipice and leads to a sudden lurch, as when Oedipus turns from detective to criminal.

69   Those within the faulty system exploit it to our detriment

Films like *The Big Short* have described this process. It was based on the book of that name by Michael Lewis, published by Penguin, 2011.

70   f) Work-Welfare: Facing both Ways

Paying people while they do nothing makes no sense at all, and puts them between millstones

71   G) Cambridge Analytica: The Problem with Data Mining

Before the age of the Internet editors saved us from the darkest hatreds of mankind. These are now for sale to the biggest of bigots who learn what lies are believable and excite the most people.

72. Platform companies can overpower whole nations

The present evidence is that lies disseminate far faster than truth, if only because they are more dramatic, more outlandish and bring us more rabid "friends". It is similar in this respect to religious cults. The more incredible their claims, the tighter the community of true believers who must keep communicating to maintain their beliefs.

73. h) Freedom vs responsibility: Anonymity strips Responsibility away from Freedom

If people do not own up to originating a particular message, then do not be surprised if rape fantasies involving your children while you are forced to watch fill your in-box. Only identifying those who do this can stop them. The Internet is wired into our Dark Side.

74. i) Management vs. Labour: the boat growing more unsteady

See Paul Watzlawick *The Language of Change* New York: Vintage 1977 The two sets of sailors are his image.

Notes on Part IV

75 Learning to think differently

The most coherent account of this is by Gregory Bateson *Mind and Nature: A Necessary Unity,* New York: E P Dutton, 1979; see also Naomi Klein, *This Changes Everything* New York: Penguin Books, 2014, for the political obstacles.

76 The Economy is not a God-like machine in the sky

For a comprehensive list of what is wrong with the machine model, see John Cassidy, *How Markets Fail: the logic of economic calamities.* London: Penguin, 2009

77 What it means to be alive: the vitality of the whole

See Benoit B Mandelbrot, *The (Mis)Behaviour of Markets* London: Profile Books, 2005

78 Mutuality not Cause-and-Effect

Roger Bootle, *The Trouble with Markets,* London: Nicholas Brealey, 2012

79 An Economy can be like a tree which wastes nothing

This image is elaborated from Gary Hamel and C K Prahalad *Competing for the Future,* Boston: Harvard Business School Press, 1994

80 Thinking in depth systemically

This picture is redrawn from *The Necessary Revolution*, Peter Senge, London: Nicholas Brealey, 2008

81 Adam Smith conceived of the first circle or larger whole

See *Adam Smith's Mistake* by Kenneth Lux, Boston: Shambhala Books, 2012

82   Markets are also circular: The baker

For additional reasons why Smith's homely remarks about bakers and butchers do not stand up, see *Nine Visions of Capitalism,* Charles Hampden-Turner and Fons Trompenaars op.cit. pp 37-40

83   Here is how the market is supposed to work

See *The Great Unravelling* by Paul Krugman, New York: WW Norton, 2005

84   Adam Smith's dictum is reversible

America is the largest command economy in the world, with expenditure on weaponry five times that of its nearest rival. We might well cite this as the triumph of socialism! It made weapons for two world wars, Korea, Vietnam, Iraq and the Cold War. This constituted a massive government subsidy to high tech that has never ceased.

85.   The Chinese have grasped the circular nature of wealth creation

See Ming-Jer Chen *Inside Chinese Business* Boston: Harvard Business School Press, 2003

86.   At the heart of nature is paradox: Two ways of knowing

All such issues are intelligently discussed by Fritjof Capra in *The Turning Point* New York: Simon and Schuster, 1982 see also Danah Zohar *The Quantum Self* London: Bloomsbury, 1993

87. Objects and Waves: Feng Shui and Chinese folk wisdom

Feng Shui does not withstand Western scepticism, but it does reveal that Chinese culture is comfortable with the dual reality of rocks and ripples as two different ways of thinking

88. Water logic 1, Waves operating in the frequency realm

See *Water Logic* by Edward de Bono,New York: Harper Collins 1993

89. WATER LOGIC 2, SOCIAL ENTREPRENEURSHIP AS INTERFERENCE WAVES

This is another form of *Lateral Thinking* by Edward de Bono London: Jonathan Cape, 1967

90. NATURE IS FRACTAL AND LARGELY PARADOXICAL

An excellent treatment of this issue can be found in *Turbulent Mirror* John Briggs and R David Peat Perennial Library: Harper and Row, 1989

91. FRACTALS IN THE NATURAL WORLD

James Gleick, *Chaos: The Making of a New Science,* New York, Viking, 1987

92. IS THE HUMAN CONDITION JANUS-FACED?

Arthur Koestler, *Janus: A Summing up* London: Hutchinson, 1978

93. HOW WE THINK IMPOSES ORDER 1: NORMA, THE AVERAGE WOMAN

Todd Rose, *The End of Average,* London: Penguin, 2015

94. HOW WE THINK IMPOSES ORDER 2 : THE BLIND MEN AND THE ELEPHANT

The blind men and the elephant is an ancient fable of obscure origins

95. HOW WE THINK IMPOSES ORDER 3: ABSTRACTIONS AS SHADOWS

This comes from Viktor E.Frankl in *Psychotherapy and Existentialism* Harmondsworth, Penguin, 1973

96. How stories we tell reveal the culture of a company

The less amusing or remarkable the story, the more likely it is to have a significant message, otherwise it would not be repeated. It is often an indirect form of criticism, as are cartoons stuck on walls, a form this book takes. Every story retains our attention by having a series of crises, some of which point to a moral. about the nature of the social environment

97 Churchill - see that things are hopeless yet be determined to make them otherwise

Winston was little admired between the wars and found himself on the wrong side in major disputes, over women's rights, Indian independence, and the abdication crisis etc. He misread Gandhi entirely. But he was among the first of his kind to realise that fascism was a major corruption of conservatism and had the courage to recognise the looming threat in all its enormity. The Blenheim Pup had grown up. His character was tailor-made for the crisis.

98. How Brexit cuts us into quarters

We have tried to express both sides as clearly and impartially as possible. That said we are Remainers. What lets down the Leavers is what they assume, that we live in a world of scarcity, rivalry and duels where one party or company wins and the other party or company loses and must surrender its assets. This is not so much wrong factually as undesirable and avoidable culturally. Anyone in the middle gets squeezed by both sides and warring words and televised rhetoric increase polarization and facilitate drama. Verbal fisticuffs fail to create wealth which requires us to agree with each other and with customers. Flamboyant rhetoric about Britain becoming a vassal state ill-serves wealth creation of any kind. We must stop showing off and start listening. Education and innovation are the keys to the economy of the future. One of the author's ancestors was among the five members of parliament arrested by Charles 1st. As a contemporary account put it, "Everyone drew his sword and there was not a dry eye in the house." We fear that too little has changed. It is high time we sheathed our swords and worked together in a social democracy. Hong Kong and Singapore are indeed strong economies but their virtue lies not so much in free trade and world markets but in the fusion of Chinese communitarianism and social cohesion and Britain exposing them and their products to world markets. It is this synthesis which creates wealth, not the ghost of Ayn Rand and her enthronement of selfishness.

99 "I HAVE A DREAM!"

Reconciling dilemmas, as much of this book has tried to do, is akin to being nearly but not finally torn apart.

100. WEDGWOOD

Of course, Josiah was self-interested. You do not come to be the wealthiest man of your century without this, but this was not all he was. Inventor, scientist, philanthropist, salesman, humanitarian, classicist, emancipator, intellectual and visionary. He was a very long way from the self-serving merchant that Adam Smith described and no hypocrite on the subject of the public good. Smith missed the chance to join his Theory of Moral Sentiments to his Inquiry into the Wealth of Nations. If ever there was a man with Smith's "impartial spectator" within him that insisted on doing the right thing for ethical reasons, it was a man like Wedgwood or his friend Wilberforce.

101. VOLUME 2 OF THIS BOOK ADDRESSES REMEDIES - PERICLES

Pericles built an amazing foundation on which we build in Volume 2.

Books by Charles Hampden-Turner

- *Radical Man: A Theory of Psycho-social Development* New York: Doubleday, London: Duckworth, 1971
- *From Poverty to Dignity: A strategy for poor Americans* New York: Doubleday, 1973
- *Sane Asylum: Inside the Delancey Street Foundation* San Francisco: Book Company, 1974 William Morrow & Co, 1976
- *Maps of the Mind* London, Mitchell-Beazley, 1981, New York: Macmillan, 1981
- *Gentlemen and Tradesmen* London: Routledge & Kegan Paul, 1983
- *Charting the Corporate Mind* New York: The Free Press, 1989 Oxford: Basil Blackwell, 1989
- *Shell Guides to Planning* London: Shell Centre, No. 3 1985
- *Understanding Corporate Culture*, London: Economist Intelligence Unit, 1987
- *Creating Corporate Culture*, London: Piatkus, 1994   Reading MA: Addison-Wesley, 1988
- *The Titans of Saturn* (with Bram Groen) London: Cyan, Marshall Cavendish Business, 2005
- *Teaching Entrepreneurship and Innovation* Cambridge: Cambridge University Press, 2009

Books by Charles Hampden-Turner and Fons Trompenaars

- *Riding the Waves of Culture*, Nicholas Brealey, 1991 3rd edition 2014 also McGraw-Hill in USA
- *Mastering the Infinite Game* Oxford: Capstone, 1997
- *Building Cross-cultural Competence, how to create wealth from conflicting values* Chichester, Wiley 2000
- *21 Leaders for the 21st Century*, Oxford: Capstone, 2000
- *Managing People Across Cultures* Oxford: Capstone, 2004
- *Innovating in a Global Crisis*, Oxford: Infinite Ideas Press, 2009

- *Riding the Waves of Innovation: Harness the power of global culture*: New York: McGraw-Hill, 2010
- *Nine Cultures of Capitalism*: Oxford: Infinite Ideas Press, 2016.

BOOKS BY FONS TROMPENAARS

- *Did the Pedestrian Die?* Chichester, John Wiley 2003
- *Business across Cultures* (with Peter Woolliams) Oxford, Capstone, 2004
- *Infinite Ideas Company, Managing Change Across Corporate Cultures* (with Peter Prud'homme) Chichester, Wiley 2005
- *Riding the Whirlwind of Recession* Oxford: 2007
- *Servant Leadership across cultures* (with Ed. Voerman) Oxford: Infinite Ideas, 2009
- *100+ Management Models* (with Piet Hein Coburg) Oxford: Infinite Ideas Press, 2014

BOOKS BY LINDA O'RIORDAN

- *Managing Sustainable Stakeholder Relationships* Wiesbaden: Springer, 2017
- *New Perspectives on Corporate Social Responsibility*, (Linda O'Riordan, Piotr Zmuda, Stefan Heinemann eds) Wiesbaden: Springer, 2015

9 781912 635566